D1560546

3

The **Rivers** of Florida

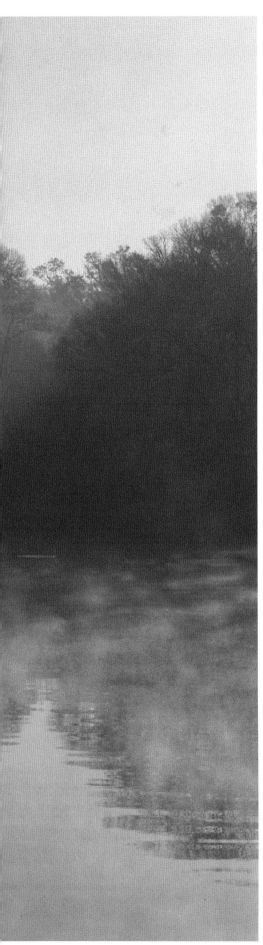

Suwannee River

The **Rivers** of Florida

Edited by Del Marth and Marty Marth

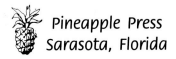

Pineapple Press
Sarasota, Florida

Most of the essays and photographs in this book originally appeared in the *Tampa Tribune*.

Photography Credits (numbers refer to pages): Robert Burke, 71; Doug Cavanah, 21; Kyle Danaceau, 29, 39; Fred Fox, 15; Mark Guss, 32, 85; Colin Hackley, 53; Tim Jackson, 61, 75; Andy Jones, 61, 64, 89; George Lane, Jr., 43; Linda L. Long, 15; Del Marth, 57; Marty Marth, 93; Jim Sherry, 25, 47; Ron Thompson, 79; Florida Department of Commerce, Division of Tourism, 47.

Published by Pineapple Press, Inc.
P.O. Drawer 16008
Southside Station
Sarasota, Florida 34239

Library of Congress Cataloging-in-Publication Data
The Rivers of Florida : essays and photographs by the staff of the
   Tampa tribune / edited by Del and Marty Marth. — 1st ed.
       p.   cm.
   "Most of the essays and photographs in this book originally
appeared in the Tampa tribune"—T.p. verso.
   ISBN 0-910923-70-1 : $24.95
   1. Rivers—Florida.   2. Rivers—Florida—Pictorial works.
3. Florida—Description and travel—1981–   4. Florida—Description
and travel—1981–   —Views.   I. Marth, Del.   II. Marth, Marty, 1947–
   III. Tampa tribune.
   F316.2.R48   1990
917.59'09593—dc20   89-49066
ISBN 0-910923-70-1   CIP

First Edition
10 9 8 7 6 5 4 3 2 1

Printed and bound in Hong Kong
Typography by E. T. Lowe, Nashville, Tennessee
Design by Joan Lange Kresek

Contents

Preface

A river, like fine
art, leaves a different impression with every
person who views it.

But unlike a Renoir or Rembrandt, Florida's rivers are subjected to development,
industry, and increasing recreational or commercial stress. In some instances, such as with the
Kissimmee River, entire routes have been
altered to suit engineers.

In 1988, the *Tampa Tribune* dispatched
writers and photographers to 18 of Florida's
major rivers to record their impressions, good
and bad. Their essays, collected in this book,
focus on whether the past two centuries have
been kind to Florida rivers and to the people
who live along those waterways.

These profiles of the state's rivers are intended to inform Floridians of the beauty, value, and fragility of our waterways. And it is
hoped that these verbal portraits will serve
as a time capsule—a mile marker—to which
future generations may refer and measure
whether they have enhanced or neglected Florida's vital natural resources.

Introduction

Florida has more than 1,700 rivers and streams. The significance of such a vast natural resource in just one state becomes clear when noting that 97 percent of the earth's water is in oceans and seas. Most of the remaining 3 percent is locked up in ice and glaciers, with less than 1 percent available as liquid fresh water, fundamental to human life. Around it, human cultures have developed. The cave men of prehistoric ages clustered around these rivers and streams. So did the ancient civilizations in Eygpt and India. And so have the urbanized, industrialized societies of our time. Florida is no exception. Without its rivers of fresh water, the state would not attract, and could not sustain, its population of more than 12 million.

But the "water wars" of Florida, like the "ranch wars" of the western states, are upon us. In 1980, Florida ranked 20th nationwide in the volume of fresh water withdrawn to serve its needs, but the state is expected to rank 9th in the year 2000. The *Water Resource Atlas* of Florida projects that by the year 2000, Florida will rank 4th (it is now 7th) in the daily volume of fresh water withdrawn for use just in the home, directly by people. As for agriculture, Florida already uses twice as much water for irrigation as all the other states east of the Mississippi River combined.

This increasing use, coupled with the pollution of the state's rivers, aquifers, and wetlands, led in 1974 to an opening salvo in the war for water in the Tampa Bay area. Pinellas County, with a population density of nearly 3,000 people per square mile, was suffering from a water shortage and saltwater intrusion of its wells. The county sought to sink wells inland, far from its boundaries, and make up its shortage by pumping fresh water out of neighboring counties.

Political boundaries may delineate governments but are not of import in meeting the demand for a necessity of life such as fresh water, a view the state has sided with. It has decreed the law allows counties to take by eminent domain the land outside their political jurisdiction needed for water supply.

But the taking of a resource from people in one part of the state by people without that resource in another part of the state is more than a legal matter; it also invokes human emotions. And thus the Florida legislature has foresightedly and energetically set up dozens of regulations and boards to prevent the fouling and waste of its fresh waters.

The profiles of Florida rivers in this volume give many clues to where the state has succeeded and where it has failed. But in nearly every case, Floridians who have lived along these rivers all their lives lament that the waters are not as clean and laden with fish as they used to be.

Some rivers such as the Econfina and the Steinhatchee, are still near their pristine state. Others, such as the mighty St. Johns and the hardworking Alafia, are nearly catatonic from abuse.

Of course, not all fresh surface water used for public supply in Florida comes from the state's rivers. But the rivers do provide 53 percent. Another 27 percent comes from lakes, and 20 percent from reservoirs. The draw on these resources would be even greater if it were not for the more than 2 million residents, or about 20 percent of the state's population, who supply their own water with private wells.

But whether the fresh water comes from

the surface or wells, all of it has its origin in the state's wetlands. They are the swamps and bogs, marshes and overflowing land, that spawn the rivers and feed the underground aquifers. Ecologically rich, the wetlands nourish the land and the animals, recharge groundwater supplies, serve as fish nurseries and rest stops for migratory birds, purify water that eventually appears in the public supply, and spawn the rivers and streams.

Often, a river is conceived only as a tiny, meandering stream dribbling from a vast swamp or marsh. Fed by tributaries, themselves of modest birth, it gently flows toward the sea, also collecting waters from springs and rain, and finally etching a channel that better defines it as a bona fide river.

A river may be one of three types—alluvial, spring-fed or blackwater—or a combination of them. Alluvial rivers carry and deposit large quantities of sediment. These rivers, such as the Apalachicola, pick up sand and deposit it as sandbars at points where the river bends. Classic alluvial rivers with their particular animal habitats, sandbars, shallows, eddies, and oxbows occur only in north Florida.

Other streams, such as the Crystal River, are intensely spring-fed and may flow directly, without looping side trips, to the sea. Spring-fed rivers are clear and provide a year-round constant temperature, which attracts manatees, spotted sea trout, and red drum.

The state's blackwater rivers are easily recognized by their dark color. Like alluvial waterways, blackwater rivers may carry some sediment and form sandbars or levees. Their darkened color arises as the rivers ebb and flow in areas of acidic flatwoods that add tannic and humic acids to the water.

The renowned Suwannee River combines all three types, but is primarily spring-fed and blackwater. In its woody origins, the Suwannee appears to be blackwater, but downstream it is fed by springs so that during dry periods it appears clear. It takes on an alluvial appearance in some areas during the wet season, when it collects sediment.

No matter the type, a river coursing toward the sea passes into a brackish transition zone between fresh and salty. The blend creates a unique and important environment. Salt stress on vegetation is relieved by the fresh water, but the water's salinity also provides an abundance of food for small crustaceans and mullusks.

The increase or decrease in salinity of an estuary also appears to signal breeding and migration patterns to a variety of species ranging from birds to crabs to sport fish. Researchers have found, for example, that the amount of fresh water discharging into the St. Lucie estuary affects the availability of nine important fish species.

Every plant and animal along a river's course plays a role in that waterway's natural balance, for each is employed by nature to provide certain functions. From microscopic plant to a large wading bird, each is linked to a chain of life: reproducing, cleaning up wastes, consuming, and being consumed. Any interruption along the chain is felt throughout the system.

We are only now refining our understanding of how these systems work. And we have learned, perhaps belatedly, that Florida's rivers are an important facet of the chain of life—not only for the smallest fish but for every Floridian as well.

For to provide its citizens a quality of life, Florida must ensure that its rivers—as well as its springs and wetlands, its lakes and aquifers—also are of quality.

Del R. Marth
Martha J. Marth
Editors

The **Rivers** of Florida

Hillsborough

by Booth Gunter

LENGTH: 54 miles.

DRAINAGE AREA: 690 square miles.

ORIGIN OF NAME: In 1769, the name Hillsborough River appeared on a British map. The river was named for the Earl of Hillsborough, Britain's colonial secretary, who controlled the pensions of the surveyors and navigators who went to the colonies. Just 12 years earlier, a Spanish explorer had christened it the River of San Julian de Arriaga. Before that, the Indians who lived in a town named Mocoso where Tampa now stands called it the Mocoso River.

TYPE: Blackwater. Like many Florida rivers, the water is tea-colored because of the tannic acid carried into it from surrounding swamps. Water quality varies from good in the upper reaches to poor in the lower reaches downtown.

CITIES ALONG THE RIVER: Tampa, Temple Terrace.

MAJOR TRIBUTARIES: Blackwater Creek, Flint Creek, New River, Trout Creek, and Cypress Creek.

SIGNIFICANCE: The Hillsborough supplies about 75 percent of the city of Tampa's drinking water. It is also used for canoeing, rowing, fishing, boating, and swimming.

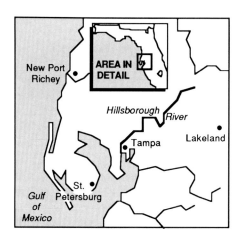

It's a spring morning on the Hillsborough River, mating season for the white ibis, and his twiggy legs and curved beak have turned a bright red in anticipation. Delicately, he pokes the mucky bottom along the edges of this blackwater river, thrusting his beak under the mud, feeling for the worms and other invertebrates that lie underneath. In a moment, the ibis is joined by three companions that burst through the high, gossamer ceiling of cypress and sweet gum. All rush downstream, full of purpose.

For these ibis, the rhythms of nature's endless cycle continue as they have for thousands of years. The wilderness of the upper Hillsborough River is their link to that untamed past, as it is for another, more intelligent species of animal—man—who has hardened the land around the lower river and harnessed the water for drinking. Indeed, a trip up the Hillsborough from Tampa is like a voyage through time, from the geometrically correct lines of the towering city through the suburbs and hardwood hammocks and cypress swamps to the primordial wilderness of the Green Swamp to the northeast.

Although modern man has occupied this territory for two centuries, only in this decade has he begun making efforts to preserve the river. Local governments are currently developing a plan to protect the river—its wilderness and its urban parts—from further urbanization and pollution. The plan is now working its way through a network of government agencies. "In the upper river, we hope to keep it just like it is, because it's magnificent," said Maxine Hatcher, chairwoman of a technical advisory committee of the Hillsborough River Interlocal

Planning Board.

This spring-fed river serves many masters. It quenches the city's ever-growing thirst for drinking water. It's a temple of serenity for canoeists escaping the hassles of the twentieth century. It's a lazy, meandering stream for fishing and a safe harbor for motorboats that buzz out into Tampa Bay and the Gulf of Mexico. It's a warm spot in winter for the friendly, whiskered manatee.

But there's an ugly side to the Hillsborough as well. The river serves as a drainage ditch for urban and agricultural runoff, responsible for high levels of fecal bacteria and other pollutants. That has caused health officials to close the river for swimming, including the famed Sulphur Springs pool. The lower river that glides through downtown Tampa now is an urban canal with concrete shorelines, carrying the city's mess into Hillsborough Bay with the falling tides. Some even complain that hoodlums threaten those fishing or boating on the river at night.

The Hillsborough has supported mankind for at least 10,000 years. The Tampa Bay area was one of the first places in Florida explored by the Spanish conquistadors, who ignored the rich bounty of fish and timber in an ill-fated attempt to find gold. It was here that repeated Spanish expeditions, beginning in the early 1500s, eventually ended in failure and death at the hands of Timucua and Calusa Indians.

The river rises from deep in the Green Swamp, where three other major rivers are born: the Withlacoochee, Peace, and Oklawaha. It starts—precisely where is not certain—as a trickle of rainwater splashing down a rut.

Because of its ecological significance, the Green Swamp has been designated an "area of critical state concern," meaning development of the area receives special scrutiny from government planners. To protect that source of fresh water from development, the Southwest Florida Water Management District has purchased about 53,500 acres of the 544,000-acre swamp that soaks through Pasco, Sumter, Lake, and Polk counties.

In the swamp east of Zephyrhills, the not-yet river flirts with the Withlacoochee before finally finding its own southwesterly path. It wriggles 54 miles to the Gulf, dropping 80 feet in elevation and draining the rainwater from 690 square miles of land along the way.

South of Green Swamp, the Hillsborough would all but disappear during the winter dry season. But a major source of water, Crystal Springs, now a privately owned recreation area, adds 40 million gallons of pure water every day from subterranean limestone caverns. Farther south, a multitude of streams drain into the river, among them Flint Creek, Blackwater Creek, New River, Trout Creek, and Cypress Creek.

Much of the river's forested flood plain below Crystal Springs is protected from development by public ownership. The Southwest Florida Water Management District owns 17 miles of riverfront on both banks, encompassing 21,110 acres. And the state owns about 3,000 acres at Hillsborough River State Park on U.S. 301.

The water district is planning to buy another 2,300 acres and seven miles of river bank, according to Fritz Musselmann, the district's real estate director. If purchased, virutally all of the riverfront between the headwaters in Green Swamp and Interstate 75 would be publicly owned and preserved in its natural state.

Canoeists love the Hillsborough, partly because there are rapids at the state park, a rarity for Florida rivers. "They're short and the water doesn't fall very much, but it does cascade over some limestone outcroppings," said county naturalist Rob Heath.

Below the park, in an area known as Seventeen Runs, the river begins to play tricks on those who would conquer it by canoe, the only way it is navigable here. Surrounded by a wet forest of red maples, sweet gum, live oaks, and cypress, the river falls apart into narrow passages, tormenting the newcomer. When the season is dry, the channels become even narrower, just a few feet wide and inches deep. In summer, when the rains come, the water will rise up and spread out over the land.

This is a truly wild place. Brown water snakes, resembling the venomous moccasin, dangle from overhanging branches or slip silently into the water from a tree that has fallen across the river. Alligators peer warily at intruders. Wild hogs plow the banks, searching for

Hillsborough

Top: A fishing boat courses through the solitude of the river's blackwater and past decades-old, moss-draped cypress trees.

Above: Tampa's skyline hovers over the widening mouth of the Hillsborough.

Left: Perpetually feeding the river, Sulphur Springs in northwest Tampa once was both a swimming spa and a provider of stored drinking water in its distant tower.

roots and small creatures to eat. A red-shouldered hawk complains loudly while a pileated woodpecker continues hammering. Occasionally, a shaft of gilded sunlight sneaks through the windblown cover, bringing new, bright hues to the cabbage palms and thick ferns on the matted floor.

It's easy to get lost. "They used to put arrows on the trees," said Heath, canoeing the river in defiance of mosquitoes. "But the purists decided that was a no-no—that if you don't know your way through, you don't belong up in here."

The thick-stumped cypress trees, clothed in Spanish moss, rise to heights of 80 feet. They're young trees, though. The ancient ones were taken in the early 1900s by men who loaded the great trunks on trams that ran on rails from the swamp to the sawmills on drier land. "It'll take another 500 years to get it back like it was," Heath remarked.

The river is stained reddish-brown by the water that flows through the forest, collecting the tannins from the rotting vegetation. It's clear enough, though, to see skittish panfish as a canoe glides downstream.

The white ibis here have ranged far from their nesting spot on Bird Island, an Audubon sanctuary in Hillsborough Bay. "They'll do a daily migration," Heath explained. "They'll fly out in the morning and fly back at night. If you're down there at dusk, you'll see clouds of them flying in. It's really quite a sight."

Leaving Seventeen Runs, the river widens near Flint Creek, which trickles into the Hillsborough from Lake Thonotosassa to the south. You can come as far upstream as Flint Creek in a power boat, but not much farther. For just before it crosses Interstate 75, a concrete flood-control structure hunches like a guillotine over the river to cut off the flow when the river gets angry and threatens the homes of those downstream. It has been used but twice—once during Hurricane Elena in 1985. When it clamps down, the flood waters leap the south bank of the river into the Tampa Bypass Canal and eventually drain into the bay.

"This is the cork at the end of the bottle," said river resident Jack Westberry, a tournament bass fisherman and guide. "They can clamp those two gates and shut this river

down." Westberry is among a group of residents downstream who have complained that the water district is too slow to use the dam, that the water often rises within inches of their doorsteps. "I feel like sooner or later they're going to let it get into our houses," he said.

From here downriver to Tampa's Fletcher Avenue, the river banks still are virtually untouched, but the land is privately owned and many fear that development could erase what took centuries to establish. Recent housing developments, like Tampa Palms, however, have been set back from the protected river banks.

West of the interstate, going downstream, lies the portion of the river called the narrows, where the river squiggles left and right through a thin channel encased in the root-tangled banks above which rise black gums and oak trees growing out of old cypress stumps. The bass fishing here is good, especially at the end of spring, when the water drops and the fish congregate in the main channel, Westberry said. Ten-pounders are taken sometimes. Panfishing is almost always good. "We ride past deer and hogs through here," he said. "There's a lot of game. My son saw a buck and a doe swim the river up here, swam right by him."

Soon, the narrows open into Lettuce Lake, a popular park just off Fletcher Avenue. Here are herons, limpkins, egrets, and ducks. Downstream from the park, houses and docks line most of the river until it reaches Hillsborough Bay. While the river keeps much of its beauty, the bank is now secured in many places by concrete walls and riprap. Hundreds of storm sewer pipes and ditches empty their liquid refuse, dumping water that is low in oxygen and high in chemicals and nutrients that can cause algae to spread and rob the water of even more oxygen. Fishing gets poorer as the stream winds toward downtown.

Farther downstream, past Temple Terrace, the river widens into Tampa's reservoir, from which 75 percent of the city's water—about 65 million gallons each day—is drawn. At the downstream end of the reservoir, the 30th Street Dam holds back the fresh water. Below the dam, because the freshwater flow is mostly gone, the river rises and falls with the tides. Some stretches are decorated with dozens of rusted shopping carts and other debris tossed into the river. This riles Richard Seward, a lifetime resident of Tampa who has spent many happy days on the river. "Nobody cares anymore," he said.

Below the dam, Sulphur Springs still pumps 20 million gallons of 72-degree water every day into the river. Early this century, the spring was turned into a swimming pool that remained popular until it was closed in 1986 because the water gushing from the ground was polluted with fecal bacteria. Environmentalists believe that Tampa's practice of using sinkholes to store storm water is to blame for ruining the springs. The sinkholes connect underground to the honeycomb of water-bearing limestone that feeds the spring.

"Here we are with all this fresh water, and we're not treating it with the high regard that we should," said Frederica Russell, an envrionmental activist and river resident who has been pushing for the cleanup of the spring. "I've got four kids, and they all love Sulphur Springs. You get out of that and it makes you feel wonderful. I'm not going to let up until it's fixed."

Manatees, the blubbery marine mammals threatened with extinction, swim up the river in winter seeking the warmth of Sulphur Springs. But fewer and fewer come here, residents say. "We used to see 14 or 15 traveling in groups upstream," Russell said. "Then they would come back and one of them would have a baby under its arms. Now, we're lucky if we see four or five."

There are other treasures here. Snook, the prize of inshore water fishermen, come up the river as far as the dam. Large tarpon have been caught, and huge Atlantic sturgeon, now rare, once were caught commercially on the river, old-timers say. But fishing below the dam has suffered, partly because of the dam, partly because of the poor water quality. As the river meanders toward the bay, the water gets worse. Heavy metals and hydrocarbons have built up in bottom sediments. The water itself is low in oxygen needed by fish.

But there's another factor influencing the use of the river. Seward, an accomplished Tampa Bay fisherman, used to fish the river for snook at night, but not anymore. "I've almost been mugged twice, once by the Slight Avenue Bridge," Seward said. "It's kind of hard to fish there anymore unless you've got someone with you—too much meanness."

The river widens as it moves toward the city. The houses get bigger, more expensive. The boats in the marinas get larger. The land flattens and the landscaping becomes more refined.

The river is tame now. Where once the river opened in a wide, mangrove-fringed mouth, the city lies. Not a mangrove in sight, nor an ibis. ~

Apalachicola

by Paul Shukovsky

LENGTH: 105 miles.

DRAINAGE AREA: 17,200 square miles.

ORIGIN OF NAME: *Apalachicola* is an Indian word with various translations, including "land beyond," "those people living on the other side," or "friendly people."

TYPE: Alluvial, meaning it transports sediment, usually from upstream erosion of silt and clay. The water is a muddy-brown color.

CITIES ALONG THE RIVER: Chattahoochee is located near the river's source at the Jim Woodruff Dam on Lake Seminole. The dam is on the Georgia-Florida border. Other cities include Blountstown, Bristol, and Apalachicola, a port town at the river's mouth on Apalachicola Bay.

SIGNIFICANCE: The Apalachicola is of great commercial value as a major inland waterway for commercial barge traffic and as a river that supports the highly productive fishery in Apalachicola Bay. Recreational fishermen and boaters also roam the length of the river. In early American history, the Apalachicola was the scene of several significant battles.

There is a comforting, tidal rhythm to life on the Apalachicola—Florida's greatest river—where just plain folks make a living by fishing its estuary or hauling cargo on its channels. "There ain't no condominiums here," fishing guide David Palmer bragged as he pointed toward the beautiful banks of the river, which has the largest flow of any stream in the state. In fact, there are relatively few homes of any sort on its 105-mile rural run from the Georgia border to the Gulf of Mexico.

It is this isolation that has helped keep its waters clean—waters that are a vital, ecological umbilical cord to one of the most productive fisheries on earth, Apalachicola Bay. For generations, men have ventured out on the bay to harvest prodigious quantities of fin fish, crab, shrimp, and oysters.

In sharp contrast to the pristine wetlands and secluded forests that hug the Apalachicola's shore, giant reminders of man—tugboats and barges longer than a football field—meander slowly along the river, which is an important inland waterway for cargo heading to and from south Georgia.

There is nothing new about cargo traffic on the river. A century ago, the now tranquil village of Apalachicola at the river's mouth was a bustling port. Paddle-wheelers, the great-granddaddy of tugboats, populated the river, bringing thousands of bales of cotton downstream from the plantations of north Florida, Alabama, and south Georgia for shipment to New York City and Europe.

The importance of cargo vessels has declined from the days when cotton was king. But the people of Apalachicola still make their living from the river and the bay. In 1987 about 920 tugs and barges hauling products including petroleum, gravel, and grains journeyed the full length of the river.

At the helm of one tug, a Cajun captain, his voice accented like a richly spiced gumbo, calls over the marine radio to the bridge tender where the Apalachicola Northern Railroad crosses the river: "Won't you open that bridge now." His vessel, the *Cajun II*, chugs past the bridge, pushing its cargo upstream. Perhaps he is heading for Bainbridge, Georgia, on the Inland Waterway, with a load of oil for a paper mill. Or maybe he is avoiding high seas and plans to stay on the Intracoastal Waterway until reaching Panama City, where the waterway returns to the Gulf of Mexico.

The Apalachicola has heard many accents over the centuries. The first inhabitants were Indians, but Franciscan friars from Spain were the first white men to occupy the area when they began establishing missions in the mid-1600s. It was not long before competition for the lucrative fur trade brought English traders into the area. Finally, conflict among the various ethnic and national groups culminated in a catastrophe on July 17, 1816.

On a quiet bluff overlooking the river about 24 miles north of Apalachicola, the sweet aroma of honeysuckle belies 170-year-old reminders of intense violence that was described in one man's journal as "horrible beyond description." About 270 people in a British fort built during the War of 1812 were killed when a single cannon shot from an American gunboat struck a powder magazine and caused a devastating explosion. There were only 30 survivors among the black "renegade" and Indian allies of the British that were stationed there. The Fort Gadsden State Historic Site still contains remnants of the fort and can be reached by taking State Road 65 to Forest Route 129.

After the War of 1812, agriculture in the area flourished and boom times began for the village of Apalachicola in the 1830s. Cotton began coming downriver in steamboats. By 1836, more than 51,000 bales were shipped through the port, and Apalachicola became the third largest cotton port on the Gulf of Mexico, surpassed only by New Orleans and Mobile.

But the boom went bust when the Civil War began and Union forces blockaded the town. After the war, the rapid growth of railroads caused a sharp decline in the number of riverboats. It was only because so much railroad track was destroyed during the war that the paddle-wheelers stayed in operation into the 1920s.

Remnants of the grandeur of old can be found on Apalachicola's Water Street along the river bank where two cotton warehouses built in 1838 still stand. There are many other historical structures in town, including an 1840 sponge exchange, an 1838 Greek Revival home assembled with pegs, and several well preserved old homes, churches, and commercial buildings.

As the cotton industry waned, the town's pace slowed and people turned to the bay to fish for a living. Today, the fishing industry is the mainstay of the town's economy. People who do not fish for a living often are dependent in some way on the bay's bounty. Merchants cater to the fishermen's needs. And the bulk of tourism in the area involves sport fishing.

At 79 years old, commercial fisherman Spero Buzier still goes shrimping by himself and credits his robust health to breathing bay air. "I like it," Buzier said. "It's a good, healthy life. You are out in the air." But he fears for the future of the fishing industry as stormwater runoff from new development and overfishing threaten the catch. "The way it's going now, in another 10 years, you can forget about shrimping," he said.

"It's going to be all condominums," oysterman Bobby Carroll, 29, added. "I've been an oysterman since I was old enough for my daddy to put me on a boat, about 6 years old. And I'd rather work on the bay than do anything. I own my own rig, and I don't have nobody telling me what to do except my wife. That bay out there is my life. And it's the only life I want." Carroll calls the community of shrimpers and oystermen who fish Apalachicola Bay's waters "a family thing."

The family of fishermen share their treasured bay with the crewmen of the tug and pusher boats that move thousands of tons

Apalachicola

Left: This bewhiskered delicacy, a plump catfish, was hooked near the Jim Woodruff Dam at the river's northern end.

Below: Skirted by a beach, the Apalachicola—one of Florida's largest rivers—yawns broadly near the town of Bristol.

Bottom: Moored oyster boats await the start of harvest season in Apalachicola Bay, the state's most prolific oyster bed.

of cargo along the river each year. Captain Ric Corley, a master mariner, has been "running this river on and off for 30 years" piloting tugs and pusher boats. Many of the tugs are out of Louisiana, which accounts for the heavy representation of Cajuns among the tugboat captains, Corley explained.

The sinuous curves of the river, he said, make it one of the most difficult to navigate of all inland waterways. "If you can navigate the Apalachicola all the way up and all the way down without running aground, you can run any river you want," he said. "It's shallow, narrow, and it's got a lot of rock in it."

It is no easy task to push a pair of barges upriver when you consider that, when combined with the boat, they total 445 feet in length. "Some of these bends you just cannot make," Corley said. "If you get stuck, you call a lock and ask them to release a little water."

When Corley runs aground and needs to call a lock for help, it's James Gilley who answers the telephone. Gilley has spent the last 31 years at the Jim Woodruff Lock and Dam located near Chattahoochee. The dam, named after a Georgian who campaigned for navigational river development, cost $45.5 million and was completed by the U.S. Army Corps of Engineers in 1957 at the spot on the Georgia border where the Flint and Chattahoochee rivers merge to form the Apalachicola. Barge traffic from the Apalachicola River is lifted by lock to Lake Seminole and can continue to Bainbridge, Georgia, on the Flint River, or to Columbus, Georgia, on the Chattahoochee River.

"There used to be more tugs," Gilley said. "I've watched the economy go and come, and that controls barge traffic like it does everything else." The most common barge cargo passing through the lock is sand and gravel used in road construction. Fertilizer is the second most common cargo. Petroleum products follow closely behind fertilizer.

In 1987, 1,327 pleasure and commercial craft passed through Gilley's locks. "Pleasure boaters, they've got plenty of money and plenty of time," Gilley said. "And they hear about a navigable waterway and they go exploring." About 400 pleasure boats passed through the lock in 1987.

Gilley is proud of the Jim Woodruff. Statistics about the lock and dam spout from his mouth like water from the spillway: "Lake Seminole covers 37,000 acres. The Flint and Chatahoochee Rivers are both 47 miles long. It takes about 22 minutes for the entire locking operation."

But not everyone on the river is happy with the lock and dam. Just ask Lavere Walker, who was "born and raised right here 78 years ago." On most days, Walker, who lost a leg in a logging accident in 1958, can be found fishing from a dock in front of his home. The remote stilt house is near the mouth of Owl Creek on the river where it borders the Apalachicola Forest. "I'd rather be on the river than anywhere," Walker said while scratching his dog Man's ear.

Walker is a man of few words. But there is one thing that gets him going: the Jim Woodruff Lock and Dam. "If they started tearing it down an hour from now, that would suit me fine. It [the river] has changed a lot ever since they put in the dam at Chattahoochee. It ought to be torn out." Walker blames the Jim Woodruff and the Corps' continual dredging of the channel for his increasingly bad luck with a rod and reel.

Dr. Robert "Skip" Livingston, director of the Center for Aquatic Research at Florida State University, agrees with Walker. "The Army Corps' dredging of the channel is destroying the river," he said. Dredging disturbs the tiny invertebrate species that live on the bottom and make meals for game fish. "We used to have a big sturgeon and striped bass fishery. But they have been knocked out by dredging."

But Livingston does have some words of praise for the Jim Woodruff. He credits the dam with helping to keep the Apalachicola River clean by containing pollution from the Flint and Chattahoochee rivers. And despite fears that development at the mouth of the river ultimately might threaten the bay, Livingston believes that an aggressive program by state agencies of buying wetlands along the Apalachicola likely will keep the river itself relatively pristine for generations to come. ~

Kissimmee

by Lee Hinnant

LENGTH: 134 miles before the channel was constructed. The channel is 56 miles long and consistently 30 feet deep and 300 feet wide, but the dimensions of the old river varied dramatically.

DRAINAGE AREA: 3,000 square miles, from south of Orlando to Lake Okeechobee.

ORIGIN OF NAME: *Kissimmee* means "long water" and is believed by some historians to have come from the Calusa Indian language.

TYPE: Blackwater. The water is stained a dark color by the natural decay of vegetation.

SIGNIFICANCE: Historically the river has been a transportation route used by Indians and pioneers. Three U.S. Army forts were constructed along it during the Seminole Wars. Steamboats plied the river until the late 1920s. Today, its main users are recreational boaters and anglers fishing for largemouth bass.

The story of the Kissimmee is a tale of two different rivers. One is a wild and serpentine stream, the other an arrow-straight ditch called C-38.

The old river was slow and meandering; it moved water inefficiently, but it fed broad marshes that were a refuge and breeding ground for wildlife. The U.S. Army Corps of Engineers changed that by dredging the controversial C-38 canal that corrals the water, but at a price.

The Kissimmee River that once was—a valley of low marshes teeming with waterfowl—will likely never be again. The artificial canal has dried 40,000 acres of flood plains along the 100 miles of river south of Lake Kissimmee.

The canal was built in an attempt to stem flooding. The effect was like drawing a stark, straight line through an elegant S curve. It is along this giant ditch that man's influence is most evident. Twisting, turning sections of the river, once laced with dead ends, potholes, and isolated lakes, were either buried with dirt from the canal or left stagnant because most of the water now runs through the canal. Hyacinths and other water weeds were practically unknown before the channel was dug. Now, they clog and choke the old river in thick green mats.

Piled next to the canal is the dirt excavated during construction—a tall, wide band of earth that looks as out of place in an isolated marsh as the F-16 fighter jets that sometimes zoom low nearby. Instead of feeding ducks or nesting cranes, the former marshes are now home to herds of cattle.

The river was once noted internationally for its largemouth bass, but anglers have not fared as well since completion of the canal, according to the state Game and Fresh Water Fish Commission. Catches in recent years have been only as good as 1959—the worst fishing year on record before construction of the ditch.

It was once a highly productive marsh, but many water birds have abandoned the valley since the U.S. Army Corps of Engineers dug the channel. The quality of waterfowl habitat decreased by 90 percent, and the number of herons, egrets, and wood storks dropped by two-thirds, a 1980 study by the U.S. Fish and Wildlife Service showed. "I used to take duck hunters and guarantee them their limit," said Oasis Marina owner J. W. Lunsford. "I haven't even bought a duck stamp in three years."

The old Kissimmee did not contribute to the pollution of Lake Okeechobee, said Richard Coleman, a chemist and environmental consultant. But since the canal, the Kissimmee feeds the second largest lake in the country about 25 percent of its diet of nitrogen and 20 percent of its phosphorus. The river gives the big lake about 30 percent of its water and is its largest tributary.

But despite the damage to its water and surrounding marshes caused by the channel, the Kissimmee is still of vital importance. "This is the life line of south Florida," said Boyd Mounts as he watched the water gush through one of six locks along the 56-mile canal. Mounts supervises the lock tenders, who are the front line of flood control during heavy rains.

The canal was authorized by Congress at the request of Florida in 1954, seven years after a devastating hurricane caused nearly $60 million in flood damage. The ditch has eliminated nuisance flooding by holding and moving water efficiently, but a state study commission concluded in 1983 that the canal will not prevent damage from a major hurricane.

Finished in 1970 after eight years of work and at a cost of $30 million, the U.S. Army Corps of Engineers canal is the most controversial but not the first to tinker with the Kissimmee system. In 1881, Philadelphia manufacturer Hamilton Disston started clearing shipping lanes between the Kissimmee chain of lakes and the Caloosahatchee River. His

crews used four dredges based in Kissimmee to open paths for commercial steamboats. But the main river channel constructed by the Corps came exactly 100 years too late to help Disston's steamboat pilots, who worked so hard navigating the tortuous river.

Also near the turn of the century, plume hunters along the river destroyed thousands of egrets and cranes to supply materials for women's fashions of the day. After federal and state laws were passed in the early 1900s to protect the birds, their populations again soared.

Today, the state, pushed by some of the same conservation groups that protested construction of the channel, is attempting to restore some of the river's natural values, such as filtration of pollution, that were lost in favor of flood control.

The Kissimmee valley still is a remarkable expanse of green and tan that stretches for miles. Hawks, buzzards, limpkins, and bald eagles swoop across the dark water, broken occasionally by the splash of an alligator dropping from the bank. But though they've had more than 15 years to try, only a few large trees break the low profile of shrubs and grasses flanking the 30-foot-deep, 300-foot-wide channel that killed the old Kissimmee.

Some 30 miles south of State Road 60, boaters can see, smell, and even feel what the old river looked like. There, the South Florida Water Management District has placed into the canal three steel dams with notches for boats. They are the keystone of restoration attempts.

Called weirs, the dams, along with culverts, allow the old river oxbows to flow and flood marshes along a 12-mile stretch. The effect has been to breathe new life into dead marshes. During high water, that stretch of the old river is dramatic, wild and winding. There are snags, confusing turns, and dead ends that can, even in broad daylight, quickly disorient a river visitor.

Like the channel, the experiment of dams is changing the face of the river. But this time, scientists say the look is for the better. Dry land plants such as myrtle are dead or dying, and are being replaced by wetland species such as willow. Since the project began three years

Kissimmee

Top left: Powerful airboats provide efficient transportation along the Kissimmee.

Top right: The Kissimmee passes ghostly remains of a once-thriving cattle settlement on Kicco Island.

Above: The natural beauty of the Kissimmee River is evident where it courses through banks left untouched by artificial channeling.

ago, plant types have increased by 50 to 100 percent, wading birds are greater in number, and game fish are more plentiful in the restored area, scientists report. In addition, muck on the old river bottom is being pushed into the canal, leaving a sandy breeding ground for small clams and other creatures near the bottom of the food chain, said Lou Toth, a scientist with the water management district.

But it is the invisible changes that may be the most important. The Kissimmee's marshes once served as sponges to absorb nutrients such as nitrogen and phosphorus, pollutants that threaten the health of Lake Okeechobee, a major water supply for south Florida. The nutrients encourage algae blooms, which rob the water of oxygen when they decompose, harming fish and other creatures. Because the channel eliminated the periodic flooding of the spongelike marshes, the nutrients have nowhere to go except into the big lake. Worse, the drying of the marshes opened the way for increased cattle grazing; this has exacerbated the problems, especially at the southern end near Lake Okeechobee where cattle manure is a major source of pollution.

Restoration attempts, to date paid for by the state, are aimed at restoring old river flows or rewetting marshes. The water management district has called Kissimmee restoration its top priority. Florida's congressional delegation is making a unified push to secure at least $2 million in federal help. The state has plans to restore another 15-mile river run, and has a contract with a California engineer to come up with further plans to help the Kissimmee.

A recent study by environmental economist Tom Lynch found that, depending on the methods used, restoring the river could increase its economic value by more than $100 million, through enticing more users. Lynch, former chief environmental economist for the state Department of Environmental Regulation, recently called for the state and the federal governments to take a fresh look at how restoration would benefit fishing, boating, and other river uses.

Because most of the land along the river is owned in large tracts by only a few cattle farmers, development pressure on the river has not been great. Most of the new construction is on the lakes in the north river area, popular spots to begin fishing expeditions.

Marina owner Lunsford and other old hands still know how and where to find the black bass, or largemouth, which is the main attraction of the river today. Most fishing is in the ring of lakes that begin just south of Orlando and stretch about 45 miles south to the southern edge of Lake Kissimmee.

There are 34 fishing camps or marinas and 27 parks or public access areas in the Kissimmee system, making the waterway popular with recreational boaters. Naturalists also frequently comb the prairies, seeking the unusual burrowing owls that live underground and come out during the day. Others search the skies for bald eagles and carcara.

Life in the waters of the Kissimmee and in the skies above it may not be as abundant as it once was. But the river, in spite of its surgical scars, remains an enticing and valuable waterway down the state's midsection. ~

Econfina

by Del Marth

LENGTH: 35 miles, beginning in the swamps of San Pedro Bay at the Taylor-Madison county line, and exiting from northwestern Taylor County into the Gulf of Mexico.

DRAINAGE AREA: 239 square miles.

ORIGIN OF NAME: Attributed to the early Indian tribes of Florida, the word *Econfina* translates as "earth bridge."

TYPE OF RIVER: Like the majority of Florida rivers, the Econfina is a blackwater river, meaning its waters contain concentrations of tannins and organic acids that come from surrounding swamps and pine forests.

SIGNIFICANCE: Purely recreational, mostly fishing. Its waters are too shallow and narrow to accommodate commercial vessels. Timber is grown along its banks by two major paper corporations.

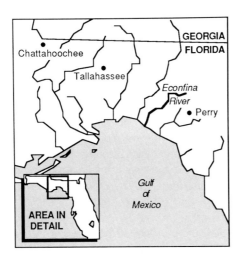

Ask the locals about the Econfina River and they all say the same thing: "It's the purest river in Florida, maybe the whole South." They may be right. No one dumps in it, mainly because only a half-dozen people live permanently along its banks. And all of them depend on the river fishing for both their livelihood and leisure. None would dare gum up the river with garbage and risk ruining a trout or mackerel season.

"You pronounce it Eee-ca-fee-nee," said Ed Sheffield, 58, looking up and down the undisturbed waterway. He has spent 40 of his years on the Econfina River, a modest run of blackwater that lollygags through Taylor County.

To mispronounce the river's name is forgivable. It is, after all, known only to a fragment of Floridians south of Perry, Taylor's county seat. In fact, the Econfina is so unimposing, so shrinking from the hustle of the rest of Florida, that only a few of the state's geologists and water-quality engineers have even been down its 35-mile route.

"It's a small, lazy stream," said Nolan Col, a program administrator with the Suwannee River Water Management District who on occasion monitors the Econfina's one surface-water gauging station. "There was talk once about a development near the fish camp. Think Buddy MacKay, the Washington politician, was in on it."

Indeed, it is more than talk these days. Politician Kenneth "Buddy" MacKay, who is from Ocala, and his brother and sister do have plans to develop two small acreage tracts along the Econfina, near its mouth. "We're planning a small motel and apartment building, and we will be selling home sites on two tracts," explained Sheffield, general manager for the MacKay family's development venture.

Albeit a small project, it is, for the reclusive Econfina River, a bold entrepreneurial move, a sort of miniature imitation of dredge-and-fill, build-and-sell capitalism. But, once done, the vision is spent. For the rest of the Econfina River's peripheral acreage—from its source in the swamps of San Pedro Bay to the marsh at its Gulf of Mexico delta—is owned by three deed-clenching land barons. They are the Buckeye Celluose Corporation, the St. Joe Paper Corporation, and the State of Florida.

For years the first two have owned sprawling timberlands along the Econfina. As for the state, it scooped up the remaining riverfront in December 1986 when it bought 62,000 acres, a transaction now famous as the Big Bend Purchase. Buckeye and St. Joe plan to continue harvesting timber along the river. But the state has more ethereal plans for its acquisition, which cost $20 million. It intends to preserve the pristine wilderness it acquired, which includes not only Econfina riverfront but the marshes and wetlands and forests along the entire coasts of Taylor and Dixie counties.

Not surprisingly, the state got very little history for its money. Hundreds of years ago, the Econfina River was as much shrouded from civilization as it is today. "At one time Indians did live along the river," said Mary Lou Whitfield, vice president of the Taylor County Historical Society. "Then, down where the Econfina meets the Gulf, is Snipe Island. Deserters from the Confederate army hid out there."

For anyone on the run, the Econfina River region made a perfect hideaway. In 1863 a detachment of Confederate cavalry tried unsuccessfully to round up the deserters in the surrounding flatwoods and cypress ponds. During their hunt, they ate sumptuously on wild deer, geese, ducks, turkeys, and hogs. But old-timers say, that without their granddaddies as guides, accompanied by hounds, the cavalry never would have found its way out.

The Econfina, despite its purity, has always been socially inhospitable. Its dimensions are not particularly inviting to settlement and commerce. "At its headwater, just east of Shady Grove, it is little more than a creek," said Rick Copeland, an administrator with the Department of Environmental Regulation. "The area, called San Pedro Bay, is flat and swampy."

Geologically, the San Pedro Bay area sits over the Floridan Aquifer, a giant underground water reservoir from which much of the state draws its water. Above the aquifer is a thick limestone formation, on which rests a bed of clay about 20 feet thick. In the Econfina region, the clay is overlain with up to 50 feet of sand.

"Although it has a current, the Econfina is real slow," said Col of the Suwannee management district. "The flow is only about 135 cubic feet per second, compared to, say, the nearby Suwannee River which is 10,000 cubic feet per second." That makes the river ideal for canoes but not for any vessel with a deep hull. Timber, for example, must be hauled out overland.

"In many places along the river one can walk across it," said Paul Miller, who manages the Econfina River Fish Camp, the only fishermen's rendezvous on the river. His camp, about two miles from the river's mouth, is situated on the MacKay tracts, one of which is 26 acres, the other 12 acres. It is here, on the river's west bank, that the breadth of the Econfina is at its widest, about 75 feet.

"There's nothing up the river from us, nor down the river," said Miller, "but it can get pretty crowded right here between April and December. That's when the fishing is best." On a good day, he said, "we'll have up to 200 boats in here. Folks from Georgia and Alabama and Tennessee, who come here for the fishing— speckled trout, Spanish mackerel, mullet. We get 'em, too, from Tampa and Leesburg and places south."

They come by word of mouth, something Sheffield is counting on to sell home sites in the two MacKay tracts. "We're talking mostly vacation homes, or second homes. Riverfront lots start at $22,000 for a quarter or half acre, and $8,000 for an upland lot," he said.

If isolation is equated with price, then the home sites are not overpriced, even for the obscure Econfina River. For traveling to the

Left: Hiding in the north Florida forests, the narrow and shallow Econfina maintains a serenity undisturbed by development and commerce.

Below left: At dawn, a fisherman pushes off into the river's slow current to replenish his larder.

Below right: A manatee, one of an estimated 1,200 still left in Florida waters, combs the river's surface for a dinner of vegetation.

Econfina Landing, as the development is called, requires leaving life, as most people know it, at Perry, on U.S. 19. Twenty miles to the west, through a vast lowland mapped out as the Aucilla Wildlife Management Area, at the end of County Road 14, the Econfina Landing is like an oasis. And fish camp manager Miller, 45, does his best to create an appropriate atmosphere. In his 60-seat restaurant, "it's all the fresh mullet and catfish you can eat," he said, which he cooks while his wife takes orders. "And we have a special at $3.95, which is you-catch-em, you-clean-em, we cook-em," he added, pointing to a fish cleaning basin next to the restaurant. "And I'll stay here cookin' till you're plum tired of eatin'."

The Econfina, and Miller, may serve up a glut of food, but the river, unlike other north Florida streams, seldom serves up an overabundance of water. Flooding, in other words, is not a problem on the Econfina. "Part of the reason," Sheffield explained, "is that excess water in San Pedro Bay flows into two other nearby rivers—the Fenholloway and the Steinhatchee." Both have their source in the San Pedro.

At the other end, the Gulf's tides are tame, providing little more than a mouthwash of briny water up to the Landing. "Although back a couple years ago," Miller said, "when Hurricane Elena came through, we had a little more water than we wanted."

It also brought into the lower Econfina more brackish water than is normal, "the only place and time the river showed any pollution," said Col.

"As I said, it's the purest river in Florida," Sheffield repeated. "And we intend to keep it that way." ~

Perpetual Attraction

The archaeological history of early Floridians reveals that people nearly always chose to settle along the state's abundant rivers. Rivers not only provided fresh water but also attracted fish and wildlife that could be hunted for food. Freshwater shellfish, snails, and mollusks appear to have been favorite Indian fare.

By the sixteenth century, Florida Indians numbered about 25,000, which anthropologists have grouped as Timucua, Tocobega, Calusa, Mayaimi, Ais, Apalachee, Apalachicola, Pensacola, and Tequesta. Seminole Indians appeared in the nineteenth century.

With the Indians came legends and myths. Nearly all tribes incorporated a water god. One such tale emanates from the Wakulla River. When under the moonlight, hundreds of little four-inch people appeared near that river's famed spring. The little people frolicked, so the legend goes, until a giant Indian warrior in a stone canoe shooed them away.

Florida was founded on the myth that a wellspring existed to ensure eternal youth to whoever drank its waters. And as for the state's rivers, they hold their own mysteries even today as streams suddenly disappear into underground oblivion, only to reappear some distance away without anyone knowing where they have been.

Old-timers knew that a series of underground caverns existed that tied into rivers, but they were not quite sure how the caverns or the water they contained behaved. One legend holds that a farmer in the Panhandle, digging a deep trench, noticed that his cow had disappeared. After searching for the animal, he thought he heard her bellow from his well. But she was certainly out of reach down there. About two weeks later, the story goes, the cow turned up. She had floated underground to the St. Marks River, then downriver to the city of St. Marks.

Manatee

by Lindsay Peterson

LENGTH: 60 miles.

DRAINAGE AREA: 129 square miles.

ORIGIN OF NAME: Named after the manatee, the water-going mammals that frequent Florida's coastal areas and inland waterways.

TYPE: Blackwater.

NEARBY COMMUNITIES: Bradenton, Palmetto, Ellenton, Parrish.

SIGNIFICANCE: The upper half of the Manatee River runs into the manmade Lake Manatee, the primary source of drinking water for Manatee and Sarasota counties. Lake Manatee is also the centerpiece of Lake Manatee State Recreational Area and open to swimmers and fishermen. The lower half of the river is used mostly for recreation such as canoeing, water skiing and fishing.

Before there were motorboats and mobile homes, before waterways became arteries of commerce and Sunday playgrounds, the Manatee River gave food and water to the Calusa and Timucuan Indians. Legend tells of a love that developed between the daughter of the Calusa chief and the son of the Timucuan chief. Their tribes lived on opposite sides of the river, and the two were forbidden to marry. So one night they ran off, meeting at a rocky spot along the river banks.

As the story goes, strange music filled the air when the two came together, and the brave believed it was an omen of good fortune. Soon after, the Calusa chief died. The tribes fought a great battle, and when many braves on both sides were slain, they agreed to merge. The couple were allowed to return to their musical river to bear the children who would rule the tribe.

The people who came later to the Manatee's banks also heard the music and they invented their own stories, said Joe and Libby Warner in their history of the Manatee, *The Singing River*. The intense, melodic humming, which has never been scientifically explained, was the wailing of a woman imprisoned by a Spanish pirate; or it was the mournful howling of a dog, killed with his owner as they strolled in the moonlight along the river banks one night.

Standing at the fabled spot today, one clearly hears a humming, whooshing sound. It's the sound of cars and trucks directly overhead on Interstate 75, racing across the three-quarter-mile mass of steel and concrete that now spans the waterway.

The history of the Manatee River is large-

Manatee

Above: Its broad, hinterland waters once a refuge for Indians and Spanish explorers, the mighty Manatee has since been bridged and dammed to accommodate miles of shoreline homes.

Right: In recent decades engineers have put the Manatee to work. This 50-foot concrete wall was built to create a reservoir of drinking water.

ly the history of Manatee County. Through its mouth at Tampa Bay came people from Maine, Ohio, Indiana—even other parts of Florida—trying to escape bad weather, ill health and Indian wars. With nineteenth-century dreams of prosperity, they settled communities that lined the waterway for 25 miles inland, from Palma Sola to Bethany. Most of their industries disappeared with the steamship, but the growth didn't stop.

When fisherman and bait seller Clyde Clyatt left Bradenton in 1942 to join the Navy, Bradenton was a small tourist haven. The city had long ago welcomed winter travelers who were shunned in Tampa, wrote the Warners, so the growth was inevitable. But when Clyatt returned in 1975, he was shocked, especially at the monopolization of the waterfront. "I've been fighting the developers ever since," he said.

Warner and his wife grew up along the river in the 1920s. To them it was a place to splash around and chase fiddler crabs. In their river history, they wrote of the excitement of the steamship days at the turn of the century. People would gather on the river banks and watch the big ships chug to and from the inland docks. But "it's changed," Joe Warner said. "And it's become more polluted as years go by."

Few spots are even accessible to the public anymore, except by boat. Homes line the waterfront downriver. "People bitch a lot if you walk through their yards," said Kevin Jenkins, 24. He is one of dozens of fishermen who head to Emerson Point in the evenings, hoping to capture a snook or two. Located where the river runs into the bay, Emerson Point is a tip of land that might soon have become inaccessible if the county hadn't recently decided to buy it. The upriver property is also private, owned largely by cattle and citrus farmers.

West of the Interstate 75 crossing, the river spreads out and heads toward the bay. To the east are miles and miles of watery avenues and cul-de-sacs. They spread through the mounds of earth, cattails, and saw grass like idle fingers extending from a winding, shaded channel. Traveling the channel upriver, the traveler would glide under overlapping oaks,

bay, pine, and palm trees. Then he would come abruptly to a 50-foot concrete wall.

That wall holds in the 7 billion gallons of water that make up the county's primary water source, Lake Manatee. Water that previously ran directly into the bay now runs through the faucets and pipes of Manatee County residents, at a rate of about 32 million gallons per day.

The water that runs into the lake begins collecting on a high plain in the northeastern edge of Manatee, near its meeting with Hillsborough, Polk, and Hardee counties. It gradually finds its way to two small streams that come together about seven miles from the east edge of the lake. The distance from the watery plain to the wide mouth is about 60 miles.

The Manatee is a river of saw grass and cattails, johnboats and Ski Nautiques, grand homes and simple cottages. To Sylvia Coleman, it's a "quiet, runny mead" as it winds slowly around the Aquatel, a shaded resort of rental cottages and canoes a few miles downriver from the dam. Coleman and her husband bought the resort about two years ago in an attempt to escape the rush of a New York executive life.

Francis Faust often travels from Sarasota to a small white sand beach downriver from the Aquatel. It's near what used to be the community of Rye, a settlement of about 75 people in the late nineteenth and early twentieth centuries.

A fishing pole rests lightly in her hands, the bobber barely moving on the surface of the tea-colored water. Maybe a catfish will bite, maybe not; either way is fine. She watches the quiet water and green, shaded banks for birds, turtles, maybe a river otter. "I said to my husband, 'Let's take a picnic and go there and sit for a while,'" she said. "It's just so peaceful and relaxing to just sit here and watch."

Years ago, farmers in the area would haul their citrus to Rye Bridge to a barge that would take the fruit downriver. They would trade the raccoons and opossums they shot along the way for goods from a commissary.

The last remaining structure in Rye burned in 1988, leaving nothing of the community but a small graveyard of defaced headstones.

Canoes and small motorboats have replaced the barges, and the Rye Bridge became known as the main swimming hole for children from the community of Parrish, said Adolph Rogers, an officer with the Florida Game and Fresh Water Fish Commission. Rogers was one of those children. Faust also brought her children there to swim. The setting hasn't changed, she said, but the water's not as clear as it was.

With the dam, the river can't clean itself as well as it used to, Rogers pointed out. Water often is released from the dam to keep the lake at a constant level, but not regularly enough to maintain a natural flow.

That worries Gloria Rains, chairman of the environmental group Manasota 88. She fears it interrupts fish breeding cycles. She also believes it may be the reason the salinity barrier between the salt and fresh water is moving further inland.

It's the litter that gets under Rogers' skin. He and his wife like to canoe down a branch of the river called Mill Creek. They often stop along the way to eat a picnic lunch, and one day, from where Rogers sat, he counted 37 discarded beer cans. "It's trashy. Trashy people."

Downriver a few miles is where resident Lindsey Hopewell learned how to swim when he fell out of a boat at the old Manatee Boat Camp. The camp, on the north shore of the river near Ellenton, is abandoned now. The elements have torn at the little cabins that are being dismantled by a developer who plans to fill the property with new homes.

Farther down the river is Fort Hamer, named in 1849 after Indian fighter General Thomas L. Hamer. Once a supply depot for government forces fighting the Seminoles, it's now known primarily as a good place to water ski because the river begins to widen but is far enough from the bay to be protected from strong winds. The strip is called "the power lines," Hopewell said. Power poles 50 feet in height strung with high-voltage lines cross over the river at that point. It's where Hopewell practices the maneuvers that won him second place at a barefoot skiing competition in Lakeland.

Getting through the creeks above and around Fort Hamer isn't easy, Hopewell said. The trick is knowing the ways of a changeable river. "It's always changing with the tides. They'll move snags and sandbars around," he explained. "That's something these people from Indiana don't realize. They think that just because they went one way one day, they can go the same way the next. They can't. They'll run aground real quick." The river isn't even charted east of the interstate because it changes so fast, Hopewell pointed out. The channel markers were made by locals for their own benefit.

Past the interstate, the river doubles in width from a quarter to a half-mile wide. Along this stretch 100 years ago were a dozen communities, including Bishop's Point, Balis' Bayou, Fogartyville, Manatee, and Ellenton. With its wealthy and ambitious settlers, Bradenton gradually became the predominant city and was bustling by 1915. It boasted 4,000 residents, several stores, a high school, telephones, and a sewer system. It thrived on the citrus money that came into the area.

But as the steamboats were replaced by the railroads, the waterfront began to lose its vibrancy, Warner explained. "As the railroad came, the docks became useless." And the waterfront businesses were replaced by residences. Gradually, the western stretch of the Manatee was lined with dwellings, from trailers to majestic homes.

The river is indeed changing, but in some very disturbing ways, say Manatee County environmental activists. The problem starts on the farmland that surrounds the river arteries that feed Lake Manatee. The water that runs into the lake is filled with nitrogen from cow manure and fertilizers. The nitrogen encourages the growth of algae, which deprives the other lake creatures of oxygen. Lake officials have tried many things: spraying with copper to stop the growth, pumping oxygen into the lake. But the problem continues.

The lake today is comparable to the dying Okeechobee in 1983, environmentalist and lifetime resident Hildegarde Bell said. Manatee County's public works department, which manages the lake, is doing everything it can, "but the river is just grossly overloaded with nutrients."

Ray Blood, superintendent of the Lake Manatee Dam, said the public works department is trying to work with the farmers to reduce the flow of fertilizers into the lake. But the farmers also are asking for a zoning change in the area to allow more houses to be built per acre. This increases the value of the land.

More people would only make the problem worse, said Bell, who finds herself up against these farmers at county commission meetings. But to her, the farmers aren't just adversaries in an issue. They're the people she grew up with. "It's hard to be pitted against old friends like this, but I have to do what I think is right," she said.

The river has the state's most restrictive water-quality designation, Class 1. But the protection doesn't extend east of Rye Bridge, which is about two miles downriver from the dam. This leaves about 10 miles of the river unprotected, and Rains fears that dumping and residential runoff are ruining the section that flows past Bradenton into the bay.

"The river's good for everything but fishing anymore," said Clarence Byrne from Ellenton. Byrne fishes at Emerson Point sometimes for snook and redfish. "About half the people lay it to the commercial fisherman. But 20 years ago there were three times the fishermen. There wasn't all this waterfront development."

The river's namesake, the manatee, is also in short supply. Rogers said the only one he has ever seen was dead. Hopewell said he hadn't seen one for years until recently when he came upon a mother and three babies. "I'd always heard that you could swim with them," he said. So, he told how he slipped into the water and moved in their direction. About that time, the mother manatee began moving in Hopewell's direction. And she was creating a wake.

"I saw her coming toward me," he said, "and I walked on water to get back to the boat." She bumped the boat as she slid past. Hopewell didn't get back into the water. ~

St. Marks

by Marty Marth

LENGTH: 35 miles long. Source is from springs in Leon County west of Tallahassee and from Lake Miccosukee on the western edge of Jefferson County.

DRAINAGE AREA: 535 square miles.

TRIBUTARIES: The only significant tributary is the Wakulla River, which flows into the St. Marks River three miles north of where the St. Marks empties into Apalachee Bay on the Gulf of Mexico.

COURSE: Flows southwest from source in Jefferson County, through eastern Leon County into eastern Wakulla County. The river's southern 12 miles, from Natural Bridge in Leon County to Apalachee Bay, is the only navigable section.

TYPE: Spring-fed.

ORIGIN OF NAME: Probably anglicized from *San Marcos*, the name given the area by Spanish explorers.

CITIES ALONG THE RIVER: The only incorporated town on the river is St. Marks, at the junction of the Wakulla and St. Marks rivers. The smaller town of Newport is upriver from St. Marks.

SITES TO VISIT: The St. Marks Historical Museum, ruins of Ft. San Marcos de Apalache, the St. Marks Lighthouse, and the Civil War battlefield of Natural Bridge.

SIGNIFICANCE: Northern navigable region is recreational, primarily fishing and boating. Two miles north from the junction of Wakulla and St. Marks is an industrial portion; heavy industries include oil refining and power plants. The entire river has great historical significance dating back to Spanish exploration, including establishment of San Marcos de Apalache, a fort built prior to 1680.

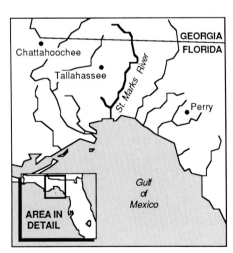

The St. Marks River has more personality quirks than its small size, a narrow 35-mile stream, deserves. At one end, it caresses canoes in its tranquil canopied and shallow waters; at the other, flexing its depths, it accommodates unsightly oil barges. Assaulted for centuries by Indians and European explorers, by the Seminole Wars and the Civil War, the St. Marks has become a river with conflicting roles.

Near its source west of Lake Miccosukee, it meanders through spring-fed wetlands among red clay banks and flat swampland. A few miles downstream, south of Natural Bridge of Civil War fame, the river disappears completely, only to resurface into a jagged rock rapids a half-mile farther south. For boaters and fishermen, the few miles below the whitewater is the end of their St. Marks, the portion of the river that has been designated by the state as an "Outstanding Florida Waterway."

Ahead, not far across the Leon County line into Wakulla County, the St. Marks braces for a day of heavy work. It begins about three miles south of a settlement called Newport, where the river is met by oil barges that are nudged by tugs along a two-mile gauntlet of industry—an oil refinery, a power plant, fuel storage and loading docks. The river isn't at peace again until it melds with the Wakulla River, merging from the west.

Most Florida rivers can boast of an undisturbed past prior to the boom days of the 1920s. Not the St. Marks. For two centuries the river has been the site of struggle, by the Indians, the Spanish, the British, then the Spanish again, even Confederate troops.

In 1528, the St. Marks beckoned Spanish explorer Narvaez, who marched overland with his troops to join ships at Apalachee Bay. Unfortunately, his ships never showed, so Narvaez and his men rigged makeshift vessels and set sail, only to perish in a Gulf storm.

Better organized Spaniards in 1679 constructed Fort San Marcos de Apalache at the crotch of land where the Wakulla and St. Marks rivers join. But peace on the river was short-lived. The Spanish were forced to yield the fort to pirates and Indians in the 1700s. Then the British took San Marcos in 1763, only to cede it back to Spain 20 years later.

Forays around the St. Marks nearly created an international crisis in 1818 when Andrew Jackson seized the fort. Ol' Hickory also court-martialed two British citizens for aiding Indians and promptly executed them. Soon, Fort San Marcos was known from Washington to London to Madrid. The U.S. Congress spent 27 days debating Jackson's conduct, with the House of Representatives voting for censure.

Three years later, the St. Marks River again made the history texts. Tallahassee became a territorial capital that year, and to solidify the area's new status, the St. Marks River became a valued transportation route for cotton, slaves, timber, furs, hides, tobacco, alcohol, and mosquito netting. To light the way into the now significant economic channel, the U.S. government in 1828 built a lighthouse at the St. Marks entrance.

That beacon signaled the channel at which a 14-ship flotilla in 1865 disembarked more than 800 Federal soldiers. They marched north to capture Newport, then St. Marks in a rear attack. The ultimate goal was Tallahassee.

The effort fell short, however. Forced to cross the St. Marks River at Natural Bridge because a railroad bridge had burned down, the Confederates drove back the Union troops and saved Tallahassee. Florida's Confederate capital was the only one east of the Mississippi never captured by the Union.

It is unlikely Narvaez or Jackson or Civil War troops would recognize the St. Marks River today—with one exception: from the river's mouth northward nine miles, along its east bank, the historical stream is bounded by the 100,000-acre St. Marks National Wildlife Refuge, founded in 1931. It is the only large parcel of publicly owned land along the St. Marks. Migrating geese, bald eagles, osprey, heron, and egret—an estimated 300 species of birds—inhabit the refuge.

Tony Ward attests to nature's bounty. The 62-year-old native Wakullan has lived, fished, and hunted along the St. Marks River all his life, as did three generations of his family before him. "In the winter, the warm river water will bring in redfish, flounder, and speckled trout," he said. Some river observers even talk about the endangered manatees coming into the St. Marks River when Gulf waters turn cold.

Hunters on the upper St. Marks can sight bear and wild turkey, but Ward recalls days down on the river's lower end when the town of St. Marks echoed with more than hunters' gunshots. "I had kin who wouldn't dare let the sun set on 'em if they were in St. Marks. During the 1930s it was like *Gunsmoke* around here. On a Friday or Saturday night you'd see two or three good fights and shootings."

Ward also related how the nearby town of Newport was born in about 1850. "It was built after a tidal wave [in the 1840s] destroyed Port Leon, the first county seat. My grandmother used to tell how, after the wave hit, people's beds were stuck in the tops of tall trees. The mud was so deep that people took the fever and the town was quarantined." After the quarantine was lifted,

St. Marks

Left: The mouth of the St. Marks provides berth for oil barges whose occasional spillages have deposited oily sediments on the channel bottom.

Below: Red clay banks of the St. Marks River have beckoned humans for more than 450 years. Indians, Spanish explorers, and Civil War soldiers all marveled at the rare beauty of this waterway's upper reaches.

Newport was built and settled and eventually became a booming shipping center of 8,000 residents. The Civil War ruined its economy, but another war, World War II, resurrected it.

"The government built invasion craft there in the 1940s," Ward explained, "so in those days the town had bowling alleys and movie theaters. But after the war, the St. Joe Paper Company bought the land, tore down the homes, and planted pine trees." Now, Ward said, Newport has just "a few families" living there. The town of St. Marks, with less than 500 residents, is the most densely populated community along the entire river.

The St. Joe Paper Company was neither the first nor the last industry attracted to the banks of the St. Marks. Today, an oil refinery, several petroleum storage tanks, as well as an oil-fired power plant are situated on or near the river. These days the two-mile stretch of river between Newport and St. Marks is routinely plied by ocean-going barges carrying petroleum products. Even tankers find their way up the section of river, some so large that engineers had to dredge a turnaround basin.

Ward said there is not much pollution from the industries "outside of when there's an oil spill." And that has happened. Since 1975, there have been 26 documented oil spills in the St. Marks, according to Lawrence Olsen, marine biologist with the Department of Environmental Regulation.

The most serious spill—10,000 gallons of No. 6 fuel oil—occurred on the river in July 1978. "The Coast Guard came in and tried to track down the culprit," said John Outland of the Department of Environmental Regulation. "The Environmental Protection Agency also came in and said, 'Gosh, this stretch of the river is really nasty from the spill.' We said, 'Yeah, we know.'"

Outland claimed his department tried without success to get cleanup funds, but "as time went on, it became less and less of an interest." That same year the Department of Environmental Regulation launched a $1.4 million study to examine the effects and removal of the contaminated sediments. Outland headed up that project, which ended nearly as quickly as it began. "We spent $65,000 to determine the feasibility of removing the sedi-

ment," he said, "but it never continued because we never could find a suitable disposal area for the contaminated material."

Contamination of the St. Marks River has never been a pressing problem, according to Outland. "You can't see the sediments. But when a barge comes up the river, the river bottom gets stirred up, and the oil rises to the top and spreads out. During larger spills, the oil got into the grasses, but after a while that tends to wash away, the oil degrades, and it becomes part of the sediments again."

Nevertheless, fishing in the lower St. Marks River is nonexistent these days. The only animal life that can be found in the river's two-mile industrial stretch is "a species of marine worms that are very pollution tolerant," said Olsen. "They are the kind you find in sewage outfall areas."

Funds for regular monitoring of the St. Marks River do not exist, Outland indicated, neither for his department nor for the Northwest Water Management District. But the Army Corps of Engineers maintains the channel, so Outland is optimistic that much of the contaminated material will be removed when the Corps does a future "as-needed" maintenance dredging.

Both Outland and Northwest Water Management District hydrologist Jeff Wagner agree that the contamination damages the river's ecology. "It's not a good situation," said Outland. "Over time, the oil degrades, and in some cases the toxic effects are left for many years."

The contamination does affect the river's estuary, Wagner said, but the contamination does not reach the Floridan Aquifer, the state's greatest water reservoir. He explains that, fortunately, the aquifer, instead of taking in river water, discharges aquifer water into the St. Marks. "The problem of the river's contaminants has not been an issue at the forefront right now," Wagner said.

Although his department's 1978 restoration project was not completed, Outland said it has prompted industries along the river to be more careful. And in spite of having 74,000 cubic yards of oily mud on her skirt, the St. Marks River, at least above her waistline, still rates as one of the state's watery glamour girls. ~

Caloosahatchee

by George Lane, Jr.

LENGTH: 75 miles, beginning in Lake Okeechobee at the Moore Haven Lock and ending in the Gulf of Mexico near Punta Rassa, St. James City, Sanibel and Estero islands.

ORIGIN OF NAME: *Caloosahatchee* is an Indian word believed to mean "river of the Calusa."

DRAINAGE AREA: 1378 square miles

TYPE: Blackwater. Its waters are dark in color as the result of high concentrations of tannic and organic acids that come from the forests along its run and from its source water, Lake Okeechobee.

CITIES ALONG THE RIVER: The river flows through three counties—Glades, Hendry, and Lee—past the cities of Moore Haven, Port La Belle, La Belle, Alva, Fort Myers, and Cape Coral.

SIGNIFICANCE: The Caloosahatchee is part of the Okeechobee Waterway that traverses the southern part of the Florida peninsula via Lake Okeechobee. It is one of three parts of the waterway that connects the Atlantic Ocean with the Gulf of Mexico and is Florida's only cross-state waterway. The Caloosahatchee is classified as a canal because of its three locks. The waterway services commercial barges and recreational boats, is a public water supply source for Lee County and the city of Fort Myers, and is used heavily for agricultural irrigation. Average annual commercial traffic is about 800,000 tons and more than 35,000 passengers. Along its banks are numerous public picnic areas, camping parks, and boat ramps.

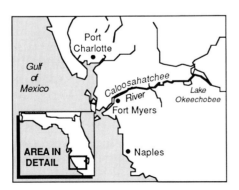

The Caloosahatchee River is an outflow of big Lake Okeechobee. This ancient, tannic acid-stained river flows westward past ranches, farms, citrus groves, towns and cities, royal palms and mangroves to its terminus in the salty Gulf of Mexico near Sanibel and Pine islands. It is best known as part of the Okeechobee Waterway, Florida's only cross-state navigable avenue for commercial and sports boaters.

Because of its three locks, the Caloosahatchee is classified as a canal. But canal, river, or ditch, and it has been called all three, it traverses a trio of counties (Hendry, Glades, and Lee), alongside five incorporated southwest Florida cities: booming Cape Coral and Fort Myers on the west, and sleepy La Belle and Moore Haven to the east.

Stretching more than 75 miles into the heartland of south Florida, the wide and narrow, muscular and moody Caloosahatchee served in the nineteenth century as a super-highway system plied by schooners and steamboats. It lured homesteaders, religious zealots, Indians, soldiers, and cattlemen, among others. A string of six crude forts stretched along its valley during the Seminole Indian Wars.

Like a sidewinder, the river serpentined westward from Lake Okeechobee through uninhabited wilderness. Over the years it and the surrounding environment have changed greatly. Today, the Caloosahatchee River is many things to many people—more than 300,000 live along its banks.

Crossed by nine highway and three railroad bridges, it is a source to two public water systems and the coolant for a large electric power plant. It is also a sanctuary for endangered manatee and an irrigation source for massive agribusiness operations. The river serves as a shipping lane as well as a recreational haven for tourists and residents.

"Part river, part canal, and part irrigation ditch, the Caloosahatchee has been long-suffering, dependable, faithful, and silent to abuses," according to long-time river watcher and supporter Robert Halgrim, a retired museum curator and friend of the late inventor Thomas A. Edison, a winter resident of Fort Myers. "For years it was an open sewer for the city of Fort Myers to dump its raw sewage, but now, thank God, that's stopped. Both Fort Myers and Lee County depend on it [above the Franklin Lock] as a water source."

According to the South Florida Water Management District, the Caloosahatchee River annually contributes more than 70 billion gallons to irrigate inland citrus groves, sugar cane fields, farm lands, and pastures. It gives more than 3 billion gallons to adjacent city and county water systems and another 300 million gallons to golf-course irrigation. The river's average daily flow is 1,332 cubic feet per second at the Franklin Lock, near Fort Myers. Both the U.S. Army Corps of Engineers and the South Florida Water Management District have jurisdiction over the Caloosahatchee and its quality, quantity, and usage.

Beyond the lake and the lock, Moore Haven is nestled on the river's north bank. The first town incorporated in the Everglades, Moore Haven was named in 1916 for founder/developer James A. Moore. Downriver, Ortona Lock, at mile marker 20.9, controls river traffic between Moore Haven and La Belle. Surrounded by ranch and farm lands, Ortona, which is Italian for "garden spot," was established as a boomtime subdivision back in the 1920s.

The river flows ever westward through sparsely populated rural country until it arrives at General Development Corporation's massive Port La Belle, a planned city and retirement area in Hendry County near LaBelle that offers a large marina, boat basin, golf course, country club, and other amenities for the rapidly growing riverside retirement community.

Moss-draped oaks and lush subtropical undergrowth dress its banks as the river reaches

the Hendry County seat town of La Belle and mile marker 30. The town's mayor, Tommy Smith, acknowledges that the river has changed, "but what hasn't in southwest Florida? The Caloosahatchee is part of our heritage. It brought many of our pioneer families here 100 years ago and it's still important to our economy." Indeed, he admits that "perhaps it is twice as important to us as others. We depend on it for transportation and irrigation, as well as for tourism."

Here and there, winding parts of the old river still can be seen between La Belle and Alva. The community of Denaud, for example, named for the French-Canadian trader Pierre Denaud, lingers amid the orange groves, pastureland, and ancient oaks along the river. During the Seminole Indian Wars, a stockade used to guard a crossing on the Caloosahatchee on the military highway between Fort Meade and Fort Myers. Today, a 1920s-vintage "swing" bridge crosses the river at the spot.

Downstream, unincorporated Alva slumbers beside the river in northeastern Lee County. It's one of the oldest settlements in the area and was founded during the steamboat era, the 1880s.

Near the Franklin Lock stands historic Olga. Once a bridge crossed the river here, but it was removed in 1969 when the lock was built. The story goes that Olga was named after a Russian princess, and the village became an overnight stop for nineteenth-century cattlemen that drove herds from inland pastures to the docks at Punta Rassa.

The river widens just above the lock at mile marker 50, the busiest lock on the river and one that provides a barrier to saltwater intrusion. Above the lock is the Lee County pumping station, the last manmade obstacle to free travel and tidal action.

Slowly, the freshwater Caloosahatchee becomes brackish and more populated, even congested. Between the State Road 31 and Interstate 75 bridges, for example, is Florida Power & Light's large Fort Myers power plant. The oil-fired steam turbine generating plant can produce up to 1,122,000 kilowatts of electrical energy during summertime peak demands. "During the winter, endangered manatees gather in the warm discharge water on FP&L's

Caloosahatchee

Below: The Caloosahatchee River is part of the Okeechobee Waterway and contains three locks, such as the Franklin near Fort Myers. Presence of the locks technically classifies the river as a canal.

Bottom: Burdened by dizzying population growth, the Caloosahatchee's mouth is veined by the mooring slips provided to charter and recreational mariners.

property and the adjacent Orange River," spokesman Gary Mehalik said. Some years nearly one-fourth of the state's vanishing manatee population (estimated to total 1,200) can be counted near the outflow.

Nearby, the CSX Railroad crosses the river at Tice. This sprawling, unincorporated community was named after its founder, Chauncey O. Tice, who settled here in the early 1900s. Then, nearing the Gulf, the slow-moving, nearly mile-wide Caloosahatchee passes Bayshore Community and reaches Fort Myers and North Fort Myers where the tides are charted and the banks are crowded with development and traffic.

Fort Myers stretches for several miles along the southern shore of the river and is the river's oldest town. Named for General Abraham Charles Myers, the fort was established in 1850 after the Seminole Wars and reactivated during the Civil War. The settlement started in about 1868 but was not incorporated until 1911. Edison built his winter home in what has been nicknamed the City of Light in 1885–86. "It was the Caloosahatchee River and its stands of bamboo that first attracted Edison here in the 1880s," said retired Edison Museum curator Halgrim. "He came here for his health, fell in love with the river and weather, had a home built and shipped here."

The inventor helped make the river and Fort Myers famous by wintering in the city and conducting synthetic rubber experiments at his Fort Myers laboratory and botanical gardens. Halgrim was a close family friend for more than 20 years. "Before the railroad was built to Fort Myers in 1904, the river was southwest Florida's only way to market its products and receive its passengers and goods," Halgrim explained. "Warehouses, packing houses, docks, and piers were ever present, in every town or settlement along its run. But railroads and hard roads replaced the steamboats and most of the river commerce." Although the river is still important to the region's agriculture, recreation, utility companies, and land development, Halgrim said that "now, as a controlled canal trained to provide a service, the river no longer is wild, untamed, and wonderful."

It is, in truth, becoming congested. An example is Cape Coral, near mile marker 70. It is the Caloosahatchee's largest city, with an estimated population of 48,000. Yet, less than forty years ago there was no Cape Coral. It was an undeveloped peninsula across the river from historic Fort Myers. Then came General Development Corporation, which developed and sold the land. Created by developers Jack and Leonard Rosen in 1958 as a planned community, Cape Coral has grown into the state's 26th most populous city, and is one of the fastest growing communities in the Southeast.

"Near where Cape Coral is today, the fish once were so thick that you could nearly walk across their backs in the river," said retired commercial fisherman B. F. Brown. "Downriver [opposite Cape Coral] we'd see redfish feeding, and it would look like 100 square yards of fish tails in the air," he said.

But the days of commercial fishing are gone. "The Caloosahatchee River and Cape Coral's system of navigable canals, combined with the assets of a planned community and excellent weather, have made Cape Coral a boom town," said chamber of commerce official Bill Roshon. But the river is a transportation barrier between northern and southern Lee County. "And there is only one bridge serving Cape Coral's growing population," Roshen pointed out.

Fort Myers and Cape Coral officials are debating the sites for a proposed new western Lee County bridge. Cost estimates range between $75 to $100 million for the four-lane, mile-long bridge. It could be 1994 to 2005 before the bridge is built.

Near the communities of St. James City on Pine Island and Punta Rassa, the old river is close to its end. The mighty Caloosahatchee dies slowly while blending its brownish waters with the blue-green Gulf of Mexico under the Sanibel Causeway.

As for the Caloosahatchee's future, it is in debate. Some say it is dead, other contend it is dying, and some say it is not even a river anymore. Most agree, however, that southwest Florida's phenomenal growth is the Caloosahatchee River's greatest problem—perhaps its greatest enemy. ~

St. Johns

by Geoffrey Mohan

LENGTH: 300 miles.

DRAINAGE AREA: 8,840 square miles.

ORIGIN OF NAME: St. Johns is the translated and shortened version of *San Juan del Puerto*, the name of the Spanish mission formerly located at the mouth of the river. Timucuan Indians called it *Welaka*, meaning "chain of lakes." The French called it *Riviere de Mai* (River of May), and it has alternately been called the San Mateo, Salamototo, and Picolata.

TYPE: Blackwater. Water is tea-colored from tannins and lignins in surrounding vegetation.

NEARBY COMMUNITIES: Melbourne, Cocoa, Titusville, Orlando, Sanford, De Land, Palatka, Jacksonville.

SIGNIFICANCE: The St. Johns is the longest river wholly in Florida and is a vital shipping channel for the port of Jacksonville. At its headwaters in Brevard and Indian River counties, the St. Johns also provides essential flood control. One of the most historically significant waterways in the state, it was explored by the Spanish and French, and hosted a thriving steamship trade that carried lumber and citrus from south Florida to the Atlantic Ocean and northern markets. It is still vital to sport fishing and recreational boating throughout its length and is one of the few major rivers on the continent that flows north in its entirety.

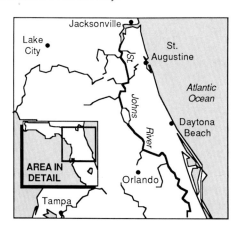

Rising from broad marshlands only 25 miles north of Lake Okeechobee, the historic St. Johns River splits the state as it flows 300 miles northward. It is a troubled river from its start. Tucked between what were prehistoric underwater ridges, the St. Johns is crimped by orange groves and fouled by sewage as it falls just over an inch per mile. By the time it flows through Jacksonville and into the Atlantic Ocean, grassy plains of marsh and cypress-pocked swamp have given way to pinched shorelines of sea walls abutted by factories and by glass and steel office buildings.

Yet for vast stretches, the river that Indians called the *Welaka*, for "chain of lakes," varies little from the description of its earliest chroniclers. In her 1889 journal *Florida Days*, poet and novelist Margaret Deland wrote of the St. Johns: "The sweep of the current is slow and grave...it is without the hurry and noise of the little running rivers of the North, and it has none of their light-hearted intimacy ...Not that the river is cruel—it is merely great; it has even an indifferent kindliness—like the ocean or the sky, or a force of nature."

Nearly everything about the river is open to argument—from who discovered it to who polluted it. Some historians say the St. Johns was discovered in 1520 by Juan Bono Quexos, who named it Rio de Corientes, or River of Currents. But others, contending that Quexos was farther north at another river, credit the French with the discovery of what they called the Riviere de Mai in 1562. The river subsequently had a succession of names like the San Mateo, Salamototo, and Picolata, but by 1821, when Spain ceded La Florida to the United States, it was known as the San Juan, named for the mission at its mouth, San Juan del Puerto.

Famed botanist and writer William Bartram placed the river in folklore with the 1791 publication of his *Travels* describing his exploration of the river as far south as Lake Harney. The book was read by English poets Coleridge and Wordsworth, who, scholars say, borrowed its images and descriptions for their poetry. Adding to that folklore was Harriet Beecher Stowe, author of *Uncle Tom's Cabin*, who moved to Mandarin, 15 miles south of Jacksonville, where she penned *Palmetto Leaves*, a paean to life on the majestic St. Johns.

More notorious Yankee residents include Mrs. W. F. Fuller, a Brooklyn native who is credited with unleashing a water hyacinth scourge on the river after snatching a sample from the New Orleans Cotton Exposition in 1884. Its beautiful purple flowers decorated the shores of her Edgewater plantation, but soon choked it so badly traffic could be "flower-locked." It remains one of the river's most serious weed problems; another is hydrilla, introduced in the 1970s.

But such folklore is forgotten in the braided and quiet stretches of the St. Johns south of Seminole County, back into the tea-dark water of Blue Cypress Lake. Most residents there bask in obscurity. "You know about heaven," said Joe Middleton, a 51-year-old former commercial fisherman who for 22 years has operated the only fish camp on the undeveloped shores of Blue Cypress Lake. "It's like they broke a piece off and left it here."

Standing on the wood porch of his Middleton Fish Camp tackle store, making beetle-spin lures to sell to local sportsmen, Middleton said, "We've had some slow times. It's up and down. I've seen some times I couldn't make it, but you just stay in it." During the busy weeks from November to March, Middleton sells up to $1,000 in fishing licenses. A busy weekend can attract 100 fishermen to the 6,550-acre lake, he said. "It's been good to us. I raised a big family out here, five children. It's been good to me—a part of my life. I get concerned too much about it. It's too high, I holler. It's too low, I holler."

Those water problems have been all too

common. Where once the headwaters consisted of 680 square miles of marsh, there are now fewer than 250 square miles, according to Dave Girardin of the St. Johns River Water Management District. Mosquito-control techniques and a land policy that rewarded landowners for every acre they drained caused problems that became apparent in the 1960s, Girardin said. The district, which already owns 28,000 acres in the St. Johns Wildlife Refuge in Orange County, is buying back 120,000 acres in the headwaters, removing dikes, and spending $124.7 million to restore the marshland.

But drainage has left Kimble "Pop" Hanna bitter. Just west of Melbourne along U.S. 192, Hanna, a self-proclaimed swamp rat and airboater, sat at the cypress bar of his fish camp, down a rutted road on the southeast side of the river. He showed yellowed articles from the *Saturday Evening Post* that told about the floating bog islands on Lake Hellen Blazes that would drift together behind the unwary boater, leaving him confounded. (It is actually Lake Hell 'n Blazes, so named for the cracker saying, "To hell 'n blazes and gone.")

"They're trying to put ten gallons of water in a five-gallon bucket," Hanna said. "I won't tell anyone a lie—I just tell it how it is. I ain't no biologist or a hydrologist. The only solution is the most logical. You put back what you took away.

"There ain't gonna be a St. Johns River. Never be another one. They way it's going now, we'll have nothing but a mudhole. Then I'll sit down and cry like a baby, then go somewhere where there's plenty of water.

"A no-legged man don't walk," he said. "A dead river don't run. If they spent half the damn money as they spent doing biological studies and bought the damn flood plain, we wouldn't have the problems we have today."

On State Road 46 in Brevard County, where the river widens and braids through grasslands before entering Lake Harney, Julia Lewis fished for bluegill from the shoreline in the Seminole Ranch Recreation Area, where the Titusville resident has come for 40 years. A white bucket beside her dilapidated orange folding chair held the day's catch, about 20 small bluegill. Her son, George Hubbard, was plucking them out and cleaning them on a

St. Johns

Top left: For all its environmental problems, the 300-mile St. Johns remains an attractive residence for ospreys.

Top right: The sightseeing vessel *Romance,* based in Sanford, transports its passengers past the oldest swinging bridge in Florida.

Above: Florida's longest river terminates at the state's most populous city, Jacksonville.

cutting board as she reeled in another eight-incher.

"I don't get here every day, but at least two, three times a week," Lewis said. On this day, she sat out rainstorms in her son's pick-up truck. She had been there since nine-thirty. I guess you could say I've been fishing forty years. I was raised in Titusville, and I been coming here since I was a kid. They're biting slow now. About two weeks ago they were bitin' so fast people were lining up. But I'll stay even if they don't bite. Sometimes I go and I don't catch anything and my kids say, 'Why you stay out there all day long?' I just say, 'Well, I love to fish.'

"The fishing is not near as good as it used to be," Lewis continued. "Now you have to go way around the river to catch specks [speckled perch], deeper holes . . . I hope they clean it [the river]. I guess it'll never get the way it used to be. I guess time changes everything."

Nature has also thrown in a quirk nearby—salt water. From Lake Poinset just west of Cocoa, to Lake Harney, west of Titusville, geological faults lying below the riverbed allow sea water from a relic ocean—a pool of trapped salt water—to bubble up, giving the river a marine character that can support blue crabs, according to Girardin. Salt water, in fact, travels in from Jacksonville to just south of Palatka, and more salt water comes from Salt Springs in the Ocala National Forest. From Palatka to Jacksonville the river is classified a marine estuary, not a river.

Farther north in Sanford, after fanning through grasslands, the river opens up into Lake Monroe, where U.S. 17 skirts seawalled shoreline dotted with new condominium projects. Rush-hour traffic clogs the road, which leads to Interstate 4 and Orlando. The St. Johns has fallen to only two feet above sea level at Sanford, once the southernmost terminus of steamboat travel. Such side- and stern-wheelers as the *Congaree, Santee, Richmond*, and *Free Trade* plied the river in the years around the Second Seminole Indian War.

In the halcyon days of steamboat travel from 1875 through the late 1880s, the DeBary-Baya Merchants Line had the biggest fleet, and regular service was offered from Savannah and Charleston to Jacksonville and points south. But by the 1930s truck traffic replaced steamboat shipping, already suffering from competition from railroads.

Otis Sloan, 76, of De Land, grew up on the riverside and can remember riding with his father in a horse-drawn wagon to the river, where steamboats delivered goods and ferried vegetable crops north to Palatka and Jacksonville. "You just give 'em an order, next morning about 8:30 they'd unload whatever you had ordered," Sloan said. "It was a damn fine river. It was clean, plenty of fishing. You could camp along the river . . . It ain't nothing but a damn septic tank now . . . I remember when I was a boy, people used to cook, swim, wash, and fish from that water.

"Yeah, this was a wonderful river back in those days. You didn't have a motor back then, just a pair of oars. Didn't have to worry about no wakes messin' you up. Didn't need no game wardens, either."

A father of four, Sloan has owned the Shady Oak Restaurant at State Road 44 for 35 years. Before that he built ocean-going tugs at the Olson shipyard in De Land and in Jacksonville and Palatka, bending the steel hulls into shape with wooden wedges and blocks. He smiled frequently and smoked constantly as he recalled the history of the river. "I've seen a lot of change," he said. "All the shell mounds, orange groves, all gone."

In the 1930s, cypress cutting began and nearly depleted the population of that tree. It ended in the late thirties, as he recalls. "That was some fine stuff," Sloan said. "Some of them logs was eight, nine foot through." Sloan recalls seeing rafts of these logs "a mile long" towed downriver to Palatka's now silent sawmills. Lumber is no longer a mainstay of Palatka's economy, but at least three large shipbuilders remain, according to Wes Larson, executive vice president of the Putnam County Chamber of Commerce.

More important to the local economy from De Land to Palatka are the bass tournaments and sport boating. The 30 miles from Lake Monroe to Lake George are dotted with 16 fish camps, lodges and restaurants, according to nautical maps posted at the Pier 44 Marine on State Road 44.

"The amount of commercial traffic has decreased," said Cheryl Corriveau, whose three-year-old River Marine Enterprises in 1987 had $1.4 million in sales at the marina. "With Orlando and that area growing, the amount of pleasure boats has increased so the weekend, well, it's just wild out there."

There are more tranquil crossings farther north. Fred and Connie Ludolff, former residents of Mars, Pennyslvania, have operated the Fort Gates Ferry from Welaka to the Ocala National Forest for 17 years. The ten-minute trip, costing $6.50 per car, can cut 54 miles from the coast to Ocala, according to Connie Ludolff. But few signs tell U.S. 17 travelers between Sanford and Palatka to turn onto County Road 309, where they will find signs leading down a three-mile packed-sand road. Nearby is the Mount Royal Indian Mound chronicled by William Bartram, where Timucuan Indians buried their dead from 1250 to 1500 A.D.

"We figure [the ferry] averages about ten cars a day," Connie Ludolff said. "Some days two or three, some days fifteen."

Six years ago, actor Paul Newman made a commercial for Datsun cars on the ferry. Ludolff treasures a photograph of Newman and the filming crew at dinner. In 1971, White Cloud toilet tissue also made a commercial on the boat. "They never showed it in Florida," she said.

As Fred Ludolff skippered a 15-foot tug hitched to the side of a 25-foot metal and wood barge, he complained of the brutal heat in the open waters stretching a half-mile wide. "It's too hot," he said. "If I had my druthers and I could move tomorrow, I'd move out of the state of Florida." After a pause, he added, "I'd go to Macon, Georgia.

"People coming on this [west] side of the river turn on their lights to let me know if they want to cross," he said, hitching the barge to the west-shore landing and lowering the ramp with a wheel and cable. His tug, made of wood on a 50-year-old hull, criss-crosses the 12-foot deep channel without major problems. "I got nuts and bolts I put on her once in a while. I don't run it full open. It gets you across. One way or the other I get to the other side."

The Fort Gates Ferry is a far cry from the river taxis that now ply the waters of the St. Johns in Jacksonville, where riverfront redevelopment has boomed. It began two years ago with Riverwalk, a boardwalk winding along the south shore of the St. Johns among riverfront cafés. Across the river, only a mile downriver from docked cargo ships and the Maxwell House coffee plant, is Jacksonville Landing. Styled like New York City's South Street Seaport, the modern glass and steel retail center just celebrated its first anniversary.

In 1988 the Jacksonville City Council passed a bond issue that includes $7 million for an additional riverwalk to complement the Jacksonville Landing. Plans are also under way to connect the riverfront to the nearby convention center via an elevated "people mover." For now, a lot of those people move via boat.

"We can carry up to 60 on board," said Jacksonville resident Mike Sanders, 35, skipper for Bass Marine Taxi Service. "Conventioneers, office people, in the evening it's predominantly people out for the evening—people using restaurants and cafés on the Riverwalk and landing."

But such developments do little for the water quality of the St. Johns, which is at its worst in Jacksonville before it fans out into the Atlantic Ocean, according to Girardin of the St. Johns River Water Management District. "Jacksonville has everything," Girardin said. "Raw sewage, heavy metals, plastics, food processing, pesticides, herbicides, fertilizers, heavy industry, oils, grease, PCBs, leads, shipping—it's got it all. Very poor water quality there."

It will be a long time before the waters of the St. Johns will pass cleanly through Jacksonville or many other areas of the state, according to Girardin. While trying to convince cities to treat sewage instead of dump it, the district is concentrating on restoring the headwaters.

"We cannot know all of the answers overnight," Girardin said. "We cannot go out and direct the major industries to do complete retro-fits. Indeed, after more than 35 years of studying this river, the process has proven to be as slow as the St. Johns itself." ~

Peace

by Brian O'Donnell

LENGTH: About 106 miles from the junction of Saddle and Peace creeks, south of Bartow, to the Charlotte Harbor estuary.

DRAINAGE AREA: 1367 square miles.

COURSE: The river mainly meanders south, curving slightly eastward below Arcadia. The river widens at Fort Ogden and is about a mile across at Punta Gorda, where it joins the estuary.

ORIGIN OF NAME: Spanish charts from the mid-1500s refer to the river as the *Rio de la Paz* (Peace River). Later maps label it Peas, or Pease, creek, leading to a contention the name stems from wild peas that once grew along its bank. In an 1842 treaty, the river was a boundary between lands claimed by Indians and settlers, giving new significance to the name Peace. Indians called it *Tolopchopko,* or "Creek of Long Peas," according to the Polk Historical Association.

TYPE: Blackwater. The water is clear but tea-colored from high concentrations of tannin and organic acids from surrounding swamps and pine forests. It is diluted by water from Lake Hancock, which is murky green from pollutants.

CITIES ALONG THE RIVER: Bartow, Fort Meade, Wauchula, Zolfo Springs, Arcadia.

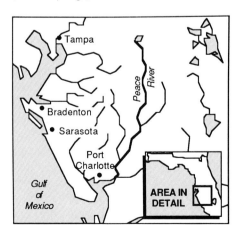

SIGNIFICANCE: Lake Hancock, the river's source, while rich in organic pollutants, supports commercial fishermen catching tilapia and catfish. River use in Hardee and De Soto counties is primarily recreaonal; canoeing, fishing, and camping are popular activities. Farther south, General Development Utilities, Inc., filters river water for drinking purposes for its Port Charlotte customers. The Peace is the largest source of fresh water in the Charlotte Harbor estuary, whose grass beds are an important breeding and spawning ground for marine life.

On a moonlit night, with palm and cypress trees reflected on the still water, crickets singing, and an occasional nightblooming moon vine flaunting its white flowers, the Peace River best lives up to its name. "This is just so relaxing, I just about can't stand it," Andy Pierce said one evening as he and his canoe meandered down the river. "You take a lazy float down the river and it's just peaceful and relaxing. That's all there is to it."

While Pierce, who runs a canoe outpost on the river, prefers to avoid the glare of the sun, the Peace River has plenty of daytime advocates. "It's a nice day," said Port Charlotte's Sandi Schwartz, who with friend Bryan Cunnigham was journeying down the Peace while enjoying a Saturday draped in a bright blue sky. "Peaceful. It's better than the beach."

But that's not the full story about this blackwater river, which gently winds more than 100 miles from Polk County to Charlotte Harbor. Because the riverbed and surrounding lands contain the valuable mineral phosphate, an ingredient in fertilizer, the Peace River and its watershed have been fighting the effects of phosphate mining nearly 100 years.

Pebbles of phosphate were discovered in the riverbed near Fort Meade in 1881, and a few years later miners were using steam-powered dredges to excavate the bottom of the Peace. The river dredging lasted about 20 years before it was replaced by more efficient strip mines inland. But the impact of phosphate continues.

Land on both sides of the river has been mined in Polk County, and the phosphate industry is slowly moving south into Hardee County. Huge amounts of wet clay produced in strip mining have spilled into the river several times, wiping out aquatic life. The most recent major spill occurred in 1980.

But the Peace River isn't all business. It is also a major source of recreation in Florida's heartland. Outdoor enthusiasts can thank Donna Stout, who moved to Arcadia in 1966 to raise cattle. She first canoed the Peace River in 1967 and fell in love with it. "We had no intention of going into the canoe business," she explained. But in 1969 she founded the Canoe Outpost with six silver vessels operating from her then-lonely homestead along the river. "We didn't see a soul on the river," Stout said. "We were there alone. It was wonderful."

The cottage where she lived with her husband and four young daughters had no running water, but the river in those days offered enough privacy for bathing. "The girls would walk down and there would be an old 'gator lazing on the bank," she said. "They would clap their hands and that old 'gator would slither away."

Canoe Outpost prospered. Now owned by Charlotte Bragg, the Outpost has 300 canoes and sends an estimated 30,000 canoeists down the river year after year. A second outfitter, Canoe Safari in Arcadia, has 180 canoes and an estimated 15,000 customers a year. And night traveler Pierce, a Sebring resident, is part owner of Peace River Canoe Excursions, a Wauchula-based operation, which has only 18 canoes.

A color brochure, "Canoe. See the real Florida," has begun attracting tourists from throughout the state, Bragg explained. The brochure is produced by the seven independently owned canoe outposts located around the state. Said Bragg, "We're getting a lot of foreign people, tourists who were at Disney World."

Canoeists come in all varieties, from the three young men from Bradenton cited by undercover wildlife officers for possession of marijuana, to seasoned campers like Tom Kingcade of West Palm Beach. Kingcade said he and his wife, Jean, were so impressed with the beauty of the Peace River they were married along its banks by a friend who is a notary public. On this Saturday afternoon, Kingcade, wearing shorts, a straw hat, and a bass-shaped necktie, reclined calmly in his canoe, which was lashed to two others occupied by friends. The makeshift flotilla, powered by a trolling motor, is complete with colorful umbrellas to provide shade for wives and two small children, and a spare canoe, containing the necessary suppies—lounge chairs, tents, a gas grill, cold beer, Maine lobster, stone crab, grouper, and steak fillets. At about four o'clock, with the pop of a champagne cork and a call of "Umbrellas down!" the Kingcade collection maneuvered toward some low-hanging trees and a flat stretch of bank, in search of a campsite for the evening.

Camping is permitted on state property along the river. The state claims ownership of the river and its shoreline to the "mean high water mark." Just what that means is unclear. Chemical companies, which mine phosphate, and the state have been fighting for years to establish where the private-public property line is. In fact, the matter is the subject of a major lawsuit, but failure to solve the issue leaves riverfront landowners like Elgin Bayless of Sebring perturbed. He is part owner of a house along the river below Zolfo Springs.

He said canoeists often use his property without permission and he's resentful over the canoe outfitters that enable too many visitors to approach his weekend retreat. "These people have completely abused these property owners and their land," he said. Canoeists cut down his trees, leave litter and smoldering

The Peace River lives up to its
name, guiding canoeists under
canopied waters much as it did
for Indians and early settlers
centuries ago.

camp fires, and have even used his driveway as a bathroom. "I look like a garbage dump," he said of his property. "Some of those people go by half drunk and they don't even know there's a house here."

Development along the Peace River in Hardee and De Soto counties is limited. There are only about two dozen houses, with most obscured from view by wild vegetation and the river's steep bank. And 27 years ago, there were no houses, recalled Dr. Jim Kendrick, a Wauchula orthodontist, who first canoed the river as an Explorer Scout. During one canoe trip, Kendrick and others found a mastodon skeleton that was later excavated by a university team. "There were very, very few peple," he said. "It's definitely not as primitive."

The Peace River is important for the water it contributes to the Charlotte Harbor estuary, explained Tom Champeau, a fish biologist with the Game and Fresh Water Fish Commission. Many marine animals need the marsh grass and brackish water of estuaries at some point in their life cycle.

But Lake Hancock, the source of Saddle Creek, which joins with Peace Creek to form the Peace River, is one of the most polluted water bodies in the state, Champeau said. Nutrients from sewage and discharge from citrus and phosphate companies make the 4,500-acre lake murky and unsuitable for many types of fish. Water flowing from the lake is further polluted by water running off agricultural land.

The amount of pollution from sewage con-

tributed by Lakeland and Winter Haven has decreased in recent years, with strict regulation by the Department of Environmental Regulation, but Lake Hancock's oxygen-depleted water remains suitable only for the hardy tilapia, or Nile perch, and catfish.

Tributaries of relatively clean water, however, dilute the pollution as the Peace River flows to the Gulf. As the water quality improves, so does the variety of marine life. Biologists have counted 43 species of fish including bass, bluegill, sunfish, gar, and catfish in the lower Peace River, Champeau said.

Near its end, the Peace River is a source of drinking water for many Charlotte County residents. Ultimately, the river water ends up in the Charlotte Harbor estuary, where the effects of long-term pollution are still unknown. "The grasses of the estuary serve as a nursery for fish, shrimp, and other organisms vital to the harbor's entire aquatic ecosystem," Champeau explained. "Loss of these grass beds, the result of excess pollution nutrients, could be disastrous."

But not everyone on the Peace River thinks in the same terms as a scientist. Instead, others savor the river's lush greenery, the herons, turtles, alligators, and the solitude. Pierce, for example, is not thinking of water analyses, hydrological studies, or the impact of phosphate on the river as he enjoys his night canoe trip. "You think 500 or 1,000 years ago, there was some Indian out here," he said, "and it probably didn't look any different." ~

Steinhatchee

by Del Marth

LENGTH: 28 miles.
DRAINAGE AREA: 586 square miles.
MAJOR TRIBUTARIES: Creeks feed the Steinhatchee along its route, the main tributaries being Eight-Mile Creek, Boggy Creek, Rocky Creek, and Kettle Creek.
COURSE: The Steinhatchee forms in Lafayette County just south of Mayo, collecting waters from a vast wetland known as Mallory Swamp. Its flow is southwest out of Lafayette County into Taylor and Dixie, two counties bordering the Gulf of Mexico. The river is the boundary line between Taylor and Dixie counties.
DEPTH: Shallow upstream, the Steinhatchee does not acquire any depth over its mostly silt bottom until it passes a shoals area eight miles from the Gulf of Mexico. Some limestone holes, estimated to be 60 feet deep, do exist in this lower part of the river. As it flows into Deadman's Bay bordering the Gulf, the river meanders around large patches of sea grass.
ORIGIN OF NAME: *Steinhatchee* is translated as "man's river." In the past 150 years, however, the river and village have been known as Hittenhatchee, Esteenhatchee, and Isteenhatchee.

TYPE: Blackwater. The Steinhatchee shows a tannic-acid color upstream, nearest the silvaculture operations of two major timber companies, Buckeye Celluose and Georgia-Pacific. As it nears the Gulf, the river loses its coffee coloring, taking on a more transparent, spring-water appearance.
CITIES ALONG THE RIVER: Only one community, Steinhatchee, borders the river. It is near the river's mouth, and although the town has developed on both the Taylor and Dixie counties' shores, most residents and businesses are on the Taylor, or north, side. An unincorporated community, Steinhatchee's population is estimated, generously, at 1,000.
SIGNIFICANCE: Purely recreational, mainly fishing. Most prevalent species are speckled trout, mullet, mackerel, and bream. Sport and commercial fishing are evenly divided. Adjacent wildlife management area provides turkey, deer, and hog hunting.

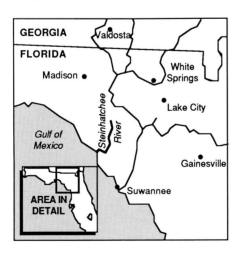

Judging Florida by its brochures showing dolphins jumping through hoops, nightly fireworks exploding over Cinderella's castle, and bikinied beauties baking on beckoning beaches, the state truly views itself as one gigantic playground. If it is that, and more than 35 million tourists each year so believe, then the Steinhatchee River is Florida's favorite fishing toy.

Fortunately, for the river's own survival, most Yankees have not yet found a road map that shows the way. But the locals, and many folks from Georgia, know how to get there. They will tell you it is not far from Rawhide Sog, after you've made the sharp turn at Knife Hammock, on the west flank of Warrior's

Swamp. Or, if coming from another direction, they advise motorists to take the short but lonely drive through Deserter's Hammock, careful to avoid being mired in Mud Swamp. Whichever, both routes are terminal, that is, they both lead to the river's end, noted on more detailed maps as Deadman's Bay.

Getting to the river's mouth, roughly between Cross City and Perry west of U.S. 19, is not like most traveling during which half the fun is the journey. In the case of the Steinhatchee River, the fun begins upon arrival, at the water's edge. As Rob Mattson, ecologist with the Suwannee River Water Management District pointed out, "The Steinhatchee is a river of recreational and wildlife values. It has no industry, no urbanization along its shores."

The fact is there is not much room for such commercial development. Compared to most Florida rivers, the Steinhatchee is only a sprint long—28 miles—and a strong-wristed fisherman can cast a line across it nearly everywhere, except perhaps at its broad mouth, a quarter-mile wide at Deadman's Bay.

Like most Florida rivers, the Steinhatchee (pronounced STEEN-hatchee) begins its journey by collecting rainwater from a vast wetland, in this case, in a soggy basin called Mallory Swamp in Lafayette County. Seeping out of Mallory, the river remains largely undefined for another 10 miles, not taking on an identity until it is bolstered by the flows from Eight-Mile Creek, Boggy Creek, Rocky Creek, and Kettle Creek. By then, however, it has left Lafayette County. It has moved on to become the political demarcation separating heavily forested Taylor County from the unpopulated lowlands of Dixie County. Then, as if preening for the flotilla of downriver fishermen, it gathers itself together and goes out of sight. "For about a mile the river disappears below ground, right around U.S. 19," said Mattson. "When it resurfaces, it does so mostly over a silt bottom. But some areas do reveal limestone rock."

One such area is a rare sight in Florida—whitewater shoals, more generously labeled a falls. Steinhatchee Falls is but a few feet high, yet it interrupts the river's quiet flow along level, pine-thickened banks. Only two other rivers in north central Florida, the Aucilla and

the Suwannee, boast similar falling waters.

It is just below Steinhatchee Falls, about eight miles from the river's mouth, that the river meets the boat traffic. For during the winter the water in this area is warm, a haven for endless schools of the Steinhatchee's most popular resident, the speckled trout. "Farther upriver, where the water is fresh, the fishing is for bream," said native Danita Deacon. "But nearer the mouth it's trout and mullet, mackerel and cobia."

The river also is again home to the endangered manatees. "Last week we had what looked like a family of four or so romping around out there," Deacon said. "It's been years since we had manatees in the river." Then she added: "I shouldn't talk about those things 'cause we might get too many people coming here. Things might get out of hand."

As it is, the one town on the river, appropriately named Steinhatchee, does get a bit of a rush during winter and spring. Hugging the Taylor County side of the river's mouth, among the sea grass and palm trees, the village is gorged during prime fishing months with visitors. "They are the people who don't care about the beaches," said Deacon. "They'd rather fish."

Just how many, no one would guess. People in Steinhatchee aren't much for counting or polling. In fact, townspeople aren't really sure how many people live in Steinhatchee. Some say around 350; others scratch their heads and pick a round number, 1,000. Come winter and spring, however, and the town's six motels and two restaurants are forced to take reservations. And waitresses at Cooey's, a famous Steinhatchee seafood emporium, agree that during the fishing season they could walk across the river just by stepping from one boat to the other.

"Most come from Georgia, some in parties and just for a weekend of fishing," said Riverside Inn owner John Lamb, who also sells real estate but prefers guiding fishing parties out of his marina.

"But we also get hunters in here," said Deacon, who works for Lamb. "We're surrounded by the Steinhatchee Wildlife Management Area. It's full of turkey and deer and hogs. Lots of folks come up from Tampa for

Steinhatchee

Full of surprises, the secretive Steinhatchee bashfully ducks underground for nearly a mile, then surfaces in a whitewater dance over shoals, and finally matures into fertile fishing grounds near the Gulf of Mexico.

hog. We call them the Tampa Hog Hunters."

For a time, both hog hunters and fisherman had difficulty getting into the town of Steinhatchee, once they had found it. Before 1948, arrivals to the south side of the river had only a two-car ferry to take them into the village. But that was solved in 1949, said Elizabeth Cooey, restaurant founder. That year, she pointed out, the town "moved a one-lane bridge here." She remembers it came from Scott's Ferry near Blountstown, "where it had been condemned."

She recalled that was the same decade that electricity came to the village, and telephones, albeit eight-party lines, were strung. In 1983 the old bridge was condemned again, so the state put in a spanking new double-lane concrete span.

Such fancy improvements eventually led to talk of newfangled ideas about protecting the environment and words such as "ecology." It got some of the more avid fishermen comparing notes about what appeared to be a decline in the fishing harvest. So they asked the Suwannee River Water Management District to check out river pollution.

"Some locals began complaining that the deep limestone holes upriver weren't providing the large catches of black drum and grouper that they were used to," said Hank Ruppertsberger, a district hydrological engineer. "They believe the deep-water holes, some of them 60 feet deep, are being filled up with sedimentation."

Of the state's five water management dis-tricts, none is so diligent as the Suwannee River district, and it began an immediate probe, primarily in the headwater basin area and along the tributaries, where much of the land is owned by Buckeye Celluose Company and Georgia-Pacific, both timber-growing companies. Ruppertsberger said the study, abetted by the two companies, is monitoring water quality and reviewing forestry operations upstream to ensure against any possible adverse runoffs into the Steinhatchee River.

Not surprisingly, old ways often still prevail along the Steinhatchee River. Commercial and sport fishing are about evenly divided, and most fishing guides are men. Women do help readying the fish for refrigerated trucking to market each day, but working the boats and marinas and equipment along the Steinhatchee is primarily men's work.

It may have something to do with the meaning of Steinhatchee, which is "man's river." Or something to do with the masculine flavor of nearby landmarks such as Deadman's Bay, an appellation harking back to piracy days that is found on eighteenth-century English maps.

Historians still write about pirate treasure being buried in the coves along the Steinhatchee River. The village people say they know nothing about it. Yet rumors persist.

Of course, it is the character of Steinhatchee folks that if they did find a cache of doubloons they wouldn't tell anybody. Along the Steinhatchee River, folks talk only about fishing. ~

Crystal

by Tom Henry

LENGTH: 7 miles.

DRAINAGE AREA: 5 square miles

ORIGIN OF NAME: Known until the mid-1800s as Weewahiiaca, from the Creek Indian words *wewa*, meaning "water", and *haiyayaka*, meaning "clear."

TYPE: Spring-fed.

CITIES ALONG THE RIVER: Crystal River, Homosassa Springs, Inverness.

SIGNIFICANCE: Considered by some biologists to be the best and most important refuge in the United States for endangered manatees. About 200 manatees—or roughly 17 percent of the 1,200 manatees believed to exist—harbor in the headwaters of the Crystal River and in the nearby Homosassa River. The river is considered a prime area for recreational boating and fishing, and its rare abundance of 30 springs attracts snorkelers from throughout Florida, the Midwest, and the Northeast.

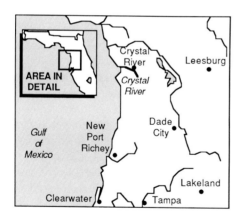

The Crystal River, a seven-mile body of water tucked away in northwest Citrus County, is a tiny package with a lot inside.

Some wildlife experts consider it the most precious manatee refuge in the United States. One reason is that it is fed by a rare abundance of 30 natural springs that pump an average of 300 million gallons of warm water into the river each day. That protects the endangered manatee from cold Gulf of Mexico waters during the winter.

Twenty-eight of the springs are in the headwaters of the river, Kings Bay. To merely call that situation unusual would be grossly underrating the uniqueness of the bay, water experts say. "In terms of an estuary system, it's probably the most unusual in the United States," said Sid Flannery, an environmental scientist with the Southwest Florida Water Management District. Waterways such as the Suwannee River have some of the same characteristics, but few places have so much to offer in such a relatively short distance.

Alligators, ducks, egrets, herons, osprey, raccoons, and otters are known to share the river with the famed manatees, a few bald eagles nest in the area from time to time, and porpoises occasionally will leave the Gulf and go up the river, said Patrick Hagan, a U.S. Fish and Wildlife official in charge of federally protected land in this part of the state. "You know how porpoises are," Hagan said. "They're kind of playful and curious. They just go up the river, take a look, and go back."

Each winter, local businessmen have counted on the Crystal River to draw hordes of tourists to see the endangered manatees.

59

And during the summer, the river has been known as a boater's paradise that offers anything from a scenic ride to great fishing. But according to environmentalists, the river now faces an uncertain future. While it is expected to remain an enjoyable place for years to come, it is facing serious threats from algae, chemical spraying, a sewage treatment plant, and waterfront development, environmentalists say.

Archaeologists have determined that Indians settled in the area about 500 B.C. and stayed for the next 16 centuries. Their diet consisted largely of oysters, and the Indians constructed huge mounds nearby. It is not known why they left.

In the 1800s and 1900s, the river fit into the town's role as a fish, oyster, and lumbering center. At one point, logs were floated down the river to a mill that produced wood slats for a New Jersey firm that was one of the country's largest pencil manufacturers.

The town named after the river was the home of David Yulee, one of Florida's first U.S. senators. Yulee, the owner of a large sugar plantation, was known for never buying or selling a slave if it meant breaking up a family. In a park nearby are ruins of a sugar mill destroyed by Union troops during the Civil War.

The Crystal River seems to have been given an appropriate name by the Indians, given the fact that its crystal-clear springs serve as the river's primary source of water. Many of the springs are referred to individually or in clusters by such colorful names as American Legion Spring, Shark Sink, Tarpon Spring, Gator Hole, Three Sisters Springs, and Idiots Delight.

Kings Bay has long served as the river's hub of activitiy and appears likely to be its center of attention for years to come. It is the bay that is the winter home of about 150 manatees, and thus a regular draw among divers throughout the United States. Although dive shop owners and motel operators say the majority of their customers come from the Tampa Bay area, they also report getting visitors from the Midwest and the Northeast who plan vacations around getting in the water to see manatees.

The bay is also the focus of the Crystal River National Wildlife Refuge, established in August 1983 when the U.S. Fish and Wildlife Service bought 33.12 acres of land from the Nature Conservancy. However, the agency views that acquisition as only one of many it is hoping to make in the years ahead to protect endangered manatees, Hagan said. Eventually, the federal government hopes to buy an additional 3,000 acres in the Crystal River area, mostly in Kings Bay.

The nearby Homosassa River, where about 50 manatees harbor each winter, is part of the Crystal River refuge. The 200 manatees that spend their winters in the refuge makes the area the fourth largest manatee refuge in the country. Fort Myers, Riviera Beach, and Port Everglades each have 225 to 300 manatees, biologists have said.

Some biologists, including Tom O'Shea of the U.S. Fish and Wildlife Service's manatee research laboratory in Gainesville, have said Kings Bay is the best manatee refuge in Florida because of its abundance of warm springs and other natural characteristics. O'Shea fears the endangered species will have little chance of survival if Kings Bay is ruined, but surveys in recent years show a steady increase in the manatee population in this part of the state. Records show the herd is four times greater than it was 20 years ago and twice as large as it was in 1978. And the 200 manatees spotted here both in the winters of 1987 and 1988 are more than a 40 percent increase over the previous high of 142 manatees spotted a few years ago.

Officials have credited public awareness, tougher boating laws, and growth management policies for the increase in numbers, but they remain cautious, fearing that more development will ruin wildlife habitat. The influx of people increases the odds of having more boats in Kings Bay, and that increases the odds of manatees being injured or killed by boat propellers.

Though some land along the bay is still in its natural state, development has been rampant enough in recent years to drive real estate prices into six-digit figures per acre. The federal government, for example, expects to pay as much as $2 milion for eight acres it wants to purchase as a site for a manatee information center.

Crystal

Left: Florida Power's Crystal River nuclear power plant looms over fishermen anchored where the river meets the Gulf of Mexico.

Above: An alligator takes an easy swim through the Crystal River.

The consensus among environmentalists is that the Crystal River has reached a fragile and pivotal moment in its history. Not only are they concerned about having wildlife habitat replaced with condominiums and restaurants, but they fear continued river pollution from chemicals and sewage effluent.

"Any kind of pollution is a concern to us," Hagan said. "Of course, the fact the manatee is there makes it more of a concern."

To some degree, algae has been a natural part of the river for years. But officials agree it has never been so abundant, and they aren't quite sure how it has gotten to be such a problem.

Crystal River City Councilwoman Helen Spivey blames the city's waste water treatment plant for much of the mess. The plant, which went on line in 1983, discharges treated sewage effluent into a canal behind City Hall. From there, the effluent goes into a creek that feeds into the bay. Spivey contends nutrients from the discharge help grow the algae and the best way to curb the situation, she says, is to upgrade the plant so that the sewage effluent can be used for spray irrigation on golf courses and lawns and other purposes that would be less threatening to the bay. But that project would cost about $2 million—and money is a big question mark in Crystal River, a city that teetered on the brink of bankruptcy less than three years ago.

"There appears to be things happening in Kings Bay that are not entirely explainable," said Richard Garrity, a district manager for the state Department of Environmental Regulation. "We have no direct evidence to indicate the plant is causing the problem in the bay. But something is happening in Kings Bay to change its character."

In 1988 the DER and the local water management district agreed the situation had become bad enough to justify studies on the bay. One study will become a set of guidelines for preserving the bay; another will attempt to pinpoint the sources of pollution.

The treatment plan could be only one of several factors. One theory is that the bay is suffering the aftermath of the 1985 Hurricane Elena, which caused flooding in the river area. The hurricane hovered about 60 miles off the Citrus County shoreline over Labor Day weekend before slamming into the Panhandle and parts of Alabama and Mississippi. Although the hurricane never actually hit Citrus County, its winds pushed salt water up the entire seven-mile length of the river and into the bay, killing hydrilla and other aquatic weeds that usually compete with algae for nutrients in the water. The theory is that the lack of vegetation allowed the algae to thrive on the river's remaining nutrients.

Although hurricanes can push an incredible amount of salt water into the Crystal River, fluctuating tidal conditions play games with the river's ecological system throughout the year, water management district scientist Flannery explained. In general, he said, Kings Bay is freshwater, but its mineral content fluctuates with the tide. The salt content of the water begins to rise just beyond Kings Bay, but some freshwater fish are able to tolerate it almost until the river reaches the Gulf. "It's a very complicated system because of the tidal condition," Flannery said. "Water is backing up on you half the time."

Many officials say the proposed river studies will prove that storm-water runoff is the biggest and most underrated polluter. Environmentalists have been calling for measures on new development to help keep the runoff from entering the bay.

Some environmentalists also claim that Citrus County is killing the bay by spraying chemicals on aquatic weeds in an attempt to keep boating channels open. They argue that the county should harvest the weeds more often with weed-eating machines and leave much of the hydrilla along the coast for manatees to feed on. But "manatees aren't enough to control it by any stretch of the imagination, especially because most of it grows during the summer, when the mammals disperse into other areas," Flannery said.

Like other Florida waterways, the Crystal River is depending largely on cool heads and lots of cash to get it through its troubled era. Spivey has hopes, too, but she's also realistic about her cleanup crusade. "I think the river could get to a situation someday where it's going to be so expensive to clean up that it's going to be ignored," she said. ∼

Aucilla

by Paul Shukovsky

LENGTH: 69 miles. The river's source is in swampy territory about nine miles north of the Georgia border in Thomas County.

DRAINAGE AREA: 747 square miles.

TRIBUTARIES: Largest tributary is the spring-fed Wacissa River, which joins the Aucilla near Nutall Rise. Other tributaries include Gum Creek, Woof Creek, Raysor Creek, Beasley Creek, Jones Mill Creek, and Cow Creek.

COURSE: The northern stretch of the Aucilla from the Georgia line to U.S. Highway 90 flows through cypress and hardwood swamp. There is no clear channel here, and the water moves in a shallow, sheet flow during wet seasons. During dry times the river almost disappears. Sneeds Smokehouse Lake at State Road 146 is one of the few locations where there is open water. Downstream from U.S. 90, the river runs along a well-defined channel. South of Lamont, the river channel plunges underground and re-emerges in a series of sinkholes. Downstream from the confluence with the Wacissa, the river channel becomes progressively broader until it reaches the Gulf of Mexico.

ORIGIN OF NAME: The word *Aucilla* is of Timucuan Indian origin, but its meaning is lost in antiquity.

TYPE: Fed by a combination of spring water and tea-colored water from wetland sources, the Aucilla is typed as a blackwater/spring-fed river.

CITIES ALONG THE RIVER: There are no major cities on the river. The tiny hamlet of Lamont in Jefferson County is the largest settlement along the Aucilla. At Nutall Rise, a few stilt homes and fish camps line the river bank.

SIGNIFICANCE: The Aucilla provides recreational opportunities for fishing and boating. Timber companies own much of the land along its shores. Some land along the river is used for cattle grazing.

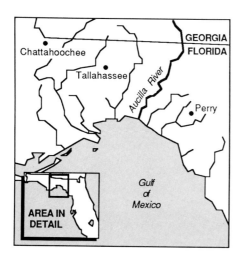

In 1925, young Wallace Blue's father fished the Aucilla River so his family could survive. Blue, now 69, still makes his home on the banks of this pristine stream in Florida's Panhandle and catches its fish like his father before him. "Me and my sister would paddle daddy down here," he said, pointing toward the river. "And we'd catch a washtub full of bream."

Blue swears it's no fish tale. The bream are still here, along with catfish, bass, and redfish. And where the Aucilla meets the Gulf of Mexico, some five miles downstream from Nutall Rise, Blue catches crab and mullet from waters that man has yet to pollute.

Such stories are increasingly rare in Florida where the pressures of people pouring into the state are rapidly eliminating precious pockets of wilderness. Helping to defend the river is a protective cocoon of wooded wetlands and pine forest owned largely by Buckeye Cel-

Aucilla

Left: One of Florida's Outstanding Waters, the Aucilla remains unspoiled by human garnishes.

Below: An occasional home or fish camp dots the Aucilla River's hem.

lulose Corporation and St. Joe Paper Company encompassing most of the Aucilla. And, at the river's mouth, the St. Marks National Wildlife Refuge is a sentinel against development. Along the banks of the Aucilla stand just a few homes on stilts and some isolated fish camps.

The river, which forms the border between Jefferson and Taylor counties, has a long history as a political boundary. From about 1100 to 1700, the Aucilla separated the Apalachee Indians from the Ustaga tribe, said John Scarry of the state's Bureau of Archaelogical Research.

Vestiges of Indian culture still can be found all along the river. The Aucilla opens its mouth wide at the Gulf into a beautiful tidal marsh. If it were not for several tiny islands covered with palm, sweet bay, and red cedar trees, the vast expanse of brown needle rush and saw grass would look like an enormous wheat field. On those islands are shards of Indian pottery, flint chips, and arrowheads.

It is a federal and state crime to remove or dig for Indian artifacts, but that does not stop some unscrupulous treasure hunters. St. Marks Refuge biologist Red Gidden has 26 years of experience at the refuge and knows several spots where the artifact thieves have struck.

His evidence is a 20-minute boat ride away from an abandoned fish camp near U.S. Highway 98. Gidden swatted a gnat away from his white beard. "Damned no-see-ums," he said and pointed the bass boat toward one of the many small islands in the marsh.

Pock marks cover the surface where artifact pirates have dug for booty. Flint chips and pottery shards lay scattered about. "They were cagey enough to put a row of brush up so people couldn't see them at work when they were passing by on the river," said Gidden with a combination of contempt and grudging admiration. He then climbed back aboard the bass boat and headed upriver.

Cormorants flee from the approaching boat, but a pair of osprey make a spectacle of themselves by performing an aerial ballet for Gidden and his companion. There are 272 species of bird found in the refuge. In the spring, Gidden stays busy making sure that turkey hunters don't end up shooting at

endangered species like the red-cockaded woodpecker.

"Occasionally, you'll see an alligator or river otter," said Gidden as the bass boat passes under the bridge at U.S. 98. The Aucilla begins to narrow here, to about 50 feet across, as Gidden proceeds upstream against the swiftly moving current.

Gidden passes a couple of fish camps and Wallace Blue's place before coming to Nutall Rise, a collection of a few small stilt houses and trailer homes. He cuts the motor so the wake will not erode docks and pilings. Then, almost like a cul-de-sac on a suburban street, the Aucilla mysteriously ends.

As in much of Florida, not far beneath the surface of the Aucilla is limestone bedrock that is riddled with chambers, passageways, and caves. The Aucilla plunges underground here at the first of what the local people call the sinks. The river simply disappears under the thick woods only to resurface several hundred yards away.

It is difficult to penetrate portions of the rugged four-mile stretch where the Aucilla boils to the surface in a series of at least 50 to 60 round sinkholes only to plunge underground again in what sometimes can be violently swirling whirlpools.

On a recent outing with a friend, wildlife officer Alton Ranew of the Florida Game and Fresh Water Fish Commission came upon one whirlpool so powerful that it was sucking logs under water. Ranew said when his friend saw the log get sucked under by the whirlpool, he started yelling for Ranew to turn the canoe around. Ranew said he needed no encouragement.

The sinks are a repository for everything that floats down the river, including Indian artifacts and fossils. Some of the deeper holes attract scuba divers who enjoy hunting for arrowheads, sharks' teeth, and mastodon bones. Wallace Blue said that just to satisfy his curiosity he dropped a line 90 feet down a sink before he ran out of rope. "There's no telling how deep they are," Blue said.

On one occasion in 1977, two young divers were hunting for artifacts and found much more than they bargained for. At a depth of about 40 feet, Lamar English, now 27, of Lake

Park, Georgia, was feeling his way through the murky water when he found himself face to face with a human skeleton. Three skeletons weighted down by concrete blocks and baling wire were found in the hole. "I didn't believe it when we saw the first body on a ledge," said English as he recalled the grisly discovery.

Lamar's friend, G. W. Pridgen, was quoted at the time as saying, "It was real weird. When we were bringing him up, it was [as] if he was smiling at us. It was almost like he was glad we had found him." It turned out the three were executed by drug smugglers at Sandy Creek the previous winter, said English, who doesn't do much diving anymore.

One of the best ways to reach the sinks is to travel by canoe down the Wacissa River, a tributary of the Aucilla that flows through Jefferson County, Ranew said. He ought to know. After six years of patrolling for the game commission, Ranew knows these woods like the back of his hand. He put in his motorized canoe at Goose Pasture campground, just a couple of miles upstream from the confluence. Goose Pasture is one of the few launch sites in the area open to the public.

White ibis, their curved beaks a dead give-away, roost atop cypress and oak, apparently oblivious to the passing boat. A stiff breeze lifts leaves, exposing the lighter shade of spring vegetation. It is in the high 60s with bright sunshine, and the reptiles are eager to warm their cold blood. The 'gators present no problem. They lie on the shore of the narrow stream sunning themselves and, with a flip of their tails, quickly swim away when the craft approaches.

Snakes are a different matter. As Ranew and his companion paddle through the log-choked channel, they pass under a lowhanging limb. "Snake!" Ranew's partner panics, pointing to a coiled critter on the limb just inches over his head. "Snake!" he yells again and prepares to attack the serpent with his paddle. "Sit still. Don't move," Ranew says. Just as the stern clears the limb, the snake drops into the water. Ranew's companion breathes a sigh of relief. Ranew is amused.

They continue their journey paddling along the narrow channel of the Wacissa until the tributary joins the Aucilla. The river is broader and deeper here, and Ranew cranks up the Evinrude.

It is startling to skim across the surface of the teacolored river and suddenly hit a dead end. On this day, there is no dramatic whirlpool at the sink. The surface is covered with logs, forest debris, and a few beer cans gently rotating as in a clogged commode.

Ranew and his companion consider traveling to the northern part of the river, but they discard the idea. At its swampy source in south Georgia some 69 miles from the Gulf and for over 30 miles to Sneeds Smokehouse Lake, the Aucilla flows in a broad, shallow sheet without a well-defined channel. The small lake is formed by a dam, Ranew says.

He turns the canoe out of the sink and motors back upstream on a broad channel that is free from logs and rocky obstructions. ~

Little Manatee

by Greg Lamm

LENGTH: 38 miles.

DRAINAGE AREA: 222 square miles.

ORIGIN OF NAME: Named after the gentle mammals that frequent Florida waters and the larger Manatee River to the south. Spanish explorers called them *manati*, referring to the handlike use of their forelimbs.

TYPE: Blackwater, caused by decaying vegetation in the river's swampy headwaters.

NEARBY COMMUNITIES: Wimauma, Sun City Center, Ruskin.

SIGNIFICANCE: Primarily recreational. The river meanders for about five miles through the Little Manatee River State Park, a wooded are of more than 1,600 acres on U.S. 301. The park has areas for picnicking, canoeing, and fishing as well as horseback riding trails. Hours year-round are 8 A.M. to sunset.

Despite a history that includes sixteenth-century European plunderers, the Little Manatee River has escaped the wrath of settlement and industry that has tainted much of Tampa Bay and its tributaries. Gangly herons and clownish pelicans continue to make a rookery of the mangrove-lined banks and land spits in the river delta. Signs posted along the river tell of swimming manatees and park boundaries. "Unspoiled" is the word most people use when they describe this river and estuary system that hooks and turns west from its swampy headwaters in rural southeastern Hillsborough County.

The Little Manatee River and nearby bays are one of the last areas on Tampa Bay where mangrove forests and sea grass beds are abundant. The area is considered the most important nursery ground for marine life in the bay. River marsh and uplands provide habitats for a number of endangered species, including the American bald eagle.

Because of this natural setting, the state Department of Environmental Regulation has designated the Little Manatee an "Outstanding Florida Water," signifying a pristine environment that should be protected from pollution. And folks like south county commercial fisherman and environmentalist Gus Muench hope it stays that way. "I wish we could keep the river looking just like this," Muench said as he powered his river-beaten crab boat past a stretch of high, sandy bank lined with palm trees and evergreens.

A red-tailed hawk soared above the 1,639-acre Little Manatee River State Park, near the U.S. 301 bridge. Ospreys stood sentry in the tops of sand pines in an area of the river that today probably looks much like it did in 1539, the year Spanish explorer Hernando de Soto and his band landed on nearby Piney Point in search of gold in the New World. "One day people will learn to appreciate these trees," said Muench, shouting above the noise of his outboard engine. "When they are all gone."

As president of the Little Manatee River Preservation Committee, Muench is leading the drive to protect the Little Manatee. But Muench's efforts are not uncontested. He faces a tough battle with real estate developers and state politicians who have a different opinion about what should be done to preserve the river and the nearby Little Cockroach and Cockroach bays.

Indeed, Muench lost the latest round in the fight for the Little Manatee. In January 1988, state Representative S. L. "Spud" Clements (D-Brandon) filed a bill that proposed to expand the Cockroach Bay Aquatic Preserve about 12 miles up the river. Local environmentalists and bay-management officials hailed the preserve expansion proposal, saying it would help preserve natural habitats along the river. But a few months later, after intense lobbying from nearby landowners, Clements removed his support for adding the river to the preserve. Instead, Clements has said he would support extending the preserve only an additional 1,500 feet into Tampa Bay. Clements's aquatic preserve expansion bill and a similar Senate bill, both without the Little Manatee addition, now must make their way through state legislative committees.

The Cockroach Bay preserve, established in 1976, includes 3,600 acres along Tampa Bay. While the state would not own additional property along the Little Manatee if the preserve were to be extended upriver, aquatic preserve designation would restrict intense development that could harm marine and bird habitats.

Clements and state Senator Malcolm Beard (R-Seffner) said they aren't convinced that development along the river would be detrimental to the environment. Both legislators said they would rather await a state study of water quality under way in the river and Cockroach Bay before deciding whether the

aquatic preserve designation upriver is necessary. "If evidence is presented to me that will show the need for further protection or regulation, the bill could be amended to reinclude the Little Manatee River in the aquatic preserve," Clements said in a letter to the *Tampa Tribune*.

Muench, who said he felt betrayed by Clements' actions, said he understands perfectly the message being sent from Tallahassee. 'I think they [Clements and Beard] are being pressured by a small group of influential people and not by a large percentage of the population," Muench said. "That bothers me."

Muench was referring to the Big Bend Area Group, a powerful coalition of property owners with 150 square miles of land along the river. But Joe Smith, the group's executive director, said Muench and other environmentalists have been unreasonable and impatient in their attempts to expand the aquatic preserve. "It is the first time I can ever remember the environmentalists saying they can't wait for a study," Smith said. "There's a struggle between the right to enjoy the property you own, which is guaranteed in the U.S. Constitution, and the powers of government to take land. This is bordering very closely on the issue of taking."

But in the years it will take state scientists to complete their study of the effects of runoff in the river, much could happen along the Little Manatee. Hillsborough County planners predict that in the early 1990s about 56,000 people will be living in the river's 220-square-mile basin in lands opened for development in 1986 when the last segment of Interstate 75 was completed nearby. In 1988 about 40,000 people lived in the river basin. If predictions are on the mark, in the next 30 years the population will swell to more than 250,000.

Like many areas of Florida, the river marshes, flatlands, and islands in the mouth of the Little Manatee were known to prehistoric Indians. On Gulf City Road, for example, archaeologists found 32 partially cremated bodies in a 60-by-60 foot burial mound and temple, according to *The WPA Guide to Florida*, a federally subsidized writers' project published during the Great Depression. And on Cockroach Key, a small island about 50 yards from shore, archaeologists found two small Indian mounds, according to the guide. In one mound, a large number of infant remains were uncovered, indicating a severe epidemic or ceremonial sacrifices. Excavations in 1936 also uncovered a shark-tooth harpoon stuck in the arm bone of an adult, according to the guide.

Lottie Castillo, 92, of Ruskin, knows about those old Indian bones. In 1912 she and her newlywed husband, fisherman Edgar Manuel Castillo, moved to the key. One morning her husband brought in a human skull and a leg bone. "I said, 'You get those things out of here,'" an animated Castillo said. "He said, 'You're living on top of a whole bunch of these.'"

Castillo delights in talking to visitors about the old days along the Little Manatee. "I thank the Lord, and I do every day, that he has given me a sound mind to tell how the river used to be." A frail but alert woman of Spanish descent with distinctive snow-white hair and dark, thick eyebrows, Castillo remembers a plentiful supply of shellfish and manatees in the river during the early part of the century. She recalls riverboats with steam-driven paddle wheels navigating waters south of "Tampa town." *The H. B. Plant*, *The Manatee*, and *The City of Sarasota* would steam by, demanding their fill of hardwood cut from a sawmill owned by Castillo's stepfather.

Castillo also remembers an old woman named Harriot Selner everybody called Grandma Selner, who was in her 70s when Castillo was a young woman. Grandma Selner told stories of the pirate Gasparilla and of Billy Bowlegs, a Seminole Indian chief who fought Colonel Zachary Taylor in the south Florida swamps during the 1830s. Bowlegs—also called Hollater-Micco—was the most famous of the Seminole warriors. He later made peace with the white settlers and settled in Hillsborough County for a while. "Grandma Selner said Billy Bowlegs sat at their table and ate many a meal," Castillo said.

Castillo had been living along the Little Manatee several years before the Dickman and Miller families moved from the Midwest to begin a new life on the eastern shores of Tampa Bay. The Dickmans were farmers; the Millers

idealists. Together they helped found Ruskin, which today is a sleepy fishing hamlet surrounded by a lucrative tomato-growing industry.

George McAnelly Miller, an attorney and college professor from Chicago, wanted a place to establish a utopian colony and school. The settlement at the mouth of the Little Manatee, known as the Ruskin Commongood Society, was named after John Ruskin, a nineteenth-century English author and critic. "The concept was that even if a family had no money, a child could get a free education, provided the child was willing to work," said Arthur "Mac" Miller, grandson of George McAnelly Miller, and a poet and professor of literature at New College in Sarasota. The society preached, among other things, individuality, equality of the sexes, and a home for everyone. The school failed, mostly due to the onset of World War I and because town fathers did not have enough municipal funds to run the city. "They were so idealistic they didn't find the power to tax income based on land sales," said Miller.

There were times, especially during the McCarthy era of the 1950s, when it was taboo for the Millers to discuss their ancestors and their socialist society for fear of reprisals, Miller said. But both families stayed in Ruskin and prospered. Today, Miller lives in the house built by A. P. Dickman near the Little Manatee River. The Dickmans became successful farmers and powerful political brokers.

Much has changed since the Dickmans and the Millers came to Florida to establish their new settlement. In the 1930s, motorists who wanted to cross Tampa Bay caught the ferry at Piney Point south of the Little Manatee River near Port Manatee. The trip to St. Petersburg by ferry took 45 minutes. A motorist was charged based on the length of his car, paying 10 cents per foot. Other passengers paid 25 cents each. Almost 60 years later, on a clear day, the thread-thin image of the Sunshine Skyway Bridge can be seen penciled in the horizon off Bahia Beach near the Little Manatee River inlet. Across the bay, downtown St. Petersburg lines the Pinellas County shore, an ominous reminder that dense development is only a few miles away.

Teams of scientists take samples of water and juvenile fish populations in and near the Little Manatee, hoping to use their results in conjunction with a state Surface Water Improvement and Management Act project to improve the waters of Tampa Bay and the Alafia and Hillsborough rivers to the north. The researchers, from the state Department of Natural Resources' Marine Resources Division in St. Petersburg, hope to be able to show the effects of storm-water runoff into the river. Storm waters can pick up pollutants from roadways, septic tanks, and chemically treated agricultural lands. When the study is completed, researchers will make nonbinding recommendations to local governments about what types of development they may want to restrict along the river.

Ken Haddad, DNR project administrator, said that while water quality in the Little Manatee is good, environmentalists and scientists should have been looking at the river 20 years ago. No data exist to show the effects development already has had on river waters. He said it's up to the people and politicians to decide if they want to preserve the Little Manatee or let its fisheries die, birds lose habitats, and water quality slip. With this study, "At least we can watch it go downhill," Haddad said.

Pessimistic? Yes, agreed Haddad, who said as a marine scientist he has watched Florida's rapid growth spoil other environmentally sensitive lands and waters. "We're used to it," he said. "We just hope [in this case] it can be minimized or controlled." ~

Little Manatee

Left: Development is the Little Manatee's prime nemesis. Population projections forecast that the river's basin will swell to more than a quarter-million people in the next 30 years.

Below left: The Little Manatee is a favorite playground for docile manatees. Signs posted along the river route urge boaters to keep a careful lookout for these marine mammals.

Below right: Lottie Castillo has lived along the Little Manatee since 1912. She fondly recalls the waterway's bountiful wildlife and how generously the river provided for its human and animal denizens.

Withlacoochee

by Rex Henderson

LENGTH: Not to be confused with the With-lacoochee River in north Florida, the "south" Withlacoochee is 86 miles long. It's headwaters are in northern Polk County at Green Swamp, which also gives rise to three other rivers—the Hillsborough, Peace, and Oklawaha—with the Withlacoochee being the longest and, in terms of water volume, the largest. The water flows east, then turns north in Pasco County, into the Withlacoochee State Forest, along the Citrus County boundary and into the estuary on the Gulf of Mexico near Yankeetown.

DRAINAGE AREA: 1,170 square miles.

ORIGIN OF NAME: The Withlacoochee was named by Indians and means "little great water."

TYPE: Blackwater.

CITIES ALONG THE RIVER: Nobleton, Dade City, Lacoochee, Dunnellon, Inglis, Yankeetown.

SIGNIFICANCE: Recreation, fishing and hunting are the major activities along the Withlacoochee. With much of the land along the river undeveloped, housing accounts for only 3 percent of the land usage, according to a document written to promote the Withlacoochee as an "Outstanding Florida Water." Some of the land in Pasco County is agricultural. Rock mining and the timber industry once flourished here, but both industries are now gone.

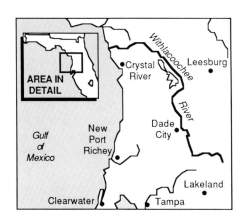

Woody Adams and the regular crowd gather early—an hour or two before noon most days—to wile away their time around picnic tables at a fishing resort hard by the Withlacoochee River. The same half-dozen weathered faces show up nearly every day, a small population of characters from varied backgrounds drawn together by the river. The river meanders in and out of their conversation, much as it meanders through the cypress swamps, pine forests, and marshes of central Florida. In snatches of talk between long silences, they discuss things that matter to this little community of river people.

A catfishing enthusiast grouses about how much better the fishing used to be. Next they may argue the merits of a landowner stringing a steel cable in an unsuccessful attempt to shut off public access to Gum Slough, a spring-fed tributary downstream. Inevitably, Adams's prowess in cleaning the turtles that are so abundant in the swamps here will also be mentioned. The turtles, like the deer, alligators, and rare birds, are nearly as plentiful now as they have ever been, Florida game specialists say.

Adams was born 70 years ago in Dunnellon on a small farm near the river. When he's talkative, he reminisces about his days as a cypress logger in the 1930s. He and a partner used a seven-foot, two-man saw to fell the huge old cypress trees and earned one dollar for every thousand linear feet of timber. For Adams, the river has been the source of his livelihood, his friend, and a lifelong companion. He says he intends to spend the rest of his life here. "I can take you up there and name you every place on this old river...the old, original names," he said proudly.

Their mutual love of the river makes friends of an unlikely pair such as Adams and Alicia Varnes, 32, an artist and a native of Homosassa, who came here from Yuma, Arizona, six years ago. She came to help her family manage Taylor Camp, but other family members eventually drifted away and left her to run the camp alone.

Varnes says the river has now cut a channel in her soul. She intends to give up the fishing camp and return to her art. But she will remain on the river, living on 10 acres of her own near Taylor Camp. "I come out here and feel new and refreshed," she said, boating down the peaceful river. "I guess it's the animal instinct in us, I don't really know. I just have to be here."

The roughhewn Taylor Camp was built about 50 years ago for the loggers who worked in what was once the major industry here. The camp is 10 miles from Inverness, the bustling Citrus County seat now caught up in a boom of development. For Adams, Varnes, and scores of river people around Taylor Camp, Inverness might as well be on another continent. Their lives move at a pace set by the Withlacoochee flowing softly past the dock.

Long stretches of the river, although privately owned, remain protected by remoteness and inaccessibility, said Jimmy Brooks, Citrus County representative on the Southwest Florida Water Management District. These lands remain today largely as they were more than 150 years ago when the Seminole Indians under Chief Osceola battled U.S. Army troops under General Duncan Clinch at a crossing near Dunnellon. The hammocks along the river were once campgrounds for thousands of Seminoles and runaway slaves who hid among the swamps and forests from the white invaders.

The river's name comes from Indian word meaning "little great water," a contradiction that speaks eloquently of the Withlacoochee. On a quiet canoe trip, the Florida that the Seminoles knew unfolds. The river's flat, glassy surface mirrors thick green tangles of cypress, oak, ash, and cedar boughs overhanging the banks, and a deep blue springtime Florida sky. It's a smoky mirror, colored by tannic acid generated by rotting vegetation in the swamps along the banks.

Turtles sun themselves on logs. An alligator's eyes and snout poke out above the water in the shallows, then sink quietly beneath the surface. Springs, hidden beneath the surface, bubble up in the swamps along the banks. A developer, before the enactment of governmental restrictions that would have stopped him today, built a dike around Blue Spring, creating a small paradise. The crystal-clear spring waters are now home to hundreds of fish and a menagerie of wildlife around the pond the developer built.

The skies are an aviary of beautiful birds. A bird watcher who spies an osprey may then find his attention claimed by great blue and great white herons, the endangered wood stork, and the handsome purple gallinule. In the winter, Varnes said, the river is host to thousands of migratory water fowl.

As the canoe glides along, she points out occasional evidence of earlier human habitation. A shack on the bank, left from the logging days, lists dangerously, nearly overgrown by the forest. Archaeologists from Gainesville come down once a year to dig through a mound at the river's edge for Indian artifacts.

For the first dozen miles or so, the Withlacoochee River is virtually indistinguishable from its origination point in the Green Swamp. It flows slowly east and then turns north in Pasco County before it first establishes a clearly defined channel.

The river flows past Dade City, and then by Lacoochee, a now impoverished settlement that was the center of the timber industry 50 years ago. North of Lacoochee, after coursing into the Withlacoochee State Forest, it flows by the Tsala Apopka chain of lakes, where the river divides into dozens of small channels and blends into the swamp. At high water the river, lakes, and swamps become a single aquatic system.

Naturalists say the river and the swamps thrive in symbiotic partnership, nourishing one another along the river's passage. The river both feeds and drains the swamps here and at the headwaters. The swamps, in turn, provide a system of natural filters for the water that runs off the uplands into the basin.

Withlacoochee

Top: Visitors turn to all types of transportation to explore the tributaries and springs of this remote river.

Above: A near-petrified cypress stump protrudes from the sun-warmed Withlachoochee, one of Florida's cleanest and best-preserved rivers.

Before the Withlacoochee dumps into the Gulf of Mexico nearly 100 miles downstream from its headwaters, the river passes through or forms the boundary of seven Florida counties: Polk, Pasco, Sumter, Hernando, Citrus, Marion, and Levy. Most of the land along the river remains undeveloped. Rock mining and the timber industry once flourished in the region, but both industries now are gone. The descendants of the miners and loggers remain in villages like Lacoochee, Istachatta, and the community around Taylor Camp. Recreation, fishing, and hunting are now the major industries along the Withlacoochee.

Other than flood-control dams, the river channel has been altered only near the Gulf, where the Inglis Dam was built in 1903 for power generation. It backs up the 3,600-acre Lake Rousseau. The hydroelectric plant has been abandoned, and the lake today is managed by the U.S. Park Service for fishing and other recreation. South of the river, a barge canal connects Lake Rousseau with the Gulf of Mexico. Kenton Lambert, a U.S. Army Corps of Engineers employee who operates the lock, said commercial users have abandoned the canal.

Twenty years ago, Brooksville, Inverness, Dunnellon, and Dade City dumped municipal sewage into the river. Citrus packers in Dade City also poured industrial waste into the river. But even at that time, the pollution in the Withlacoochee was minor compared to the contamination in the Hillsborough and the Peace rivers, said Don Moores, a chemist with the Department of Environmental Regulation in Tampa. State regulators have since eliminated or controlled those sources of Withlacoochee contamination and, Moores said, the river has recovered quickly. Today he ranks it as one of cleanest streams in west central Florida.

The Southwest Florida Water Management District, formed in 1961 for flood control, now guards the purity of the river jealously, said Brooks. Counties along its banks have recently toughened zoning rules and development regulations. Much of the land along the river is owned by the government and is protected by conservation and recreation agencies. The water district owns more than 40 miles of river and is negotiating to buy, through the state "Save Our Rivers" fund, another 8,500-acre tract in Citrus County with six miles of river frontage. The Department of Forestry controls another 13 miles of river as it runs through the Withlacoochee State Forest in Pasco, Sumter, and Hernando counties.

Still, the Southwest Florida Water Management District is tightening its control over the lands purchased with Save Our Rivers money, and efforts to preserve the river have engendered some disputes, particularly with sportsmen. The water district's aquatic weed control efforts, for example, have angered some fishermen. The district uses chemicals to kill water hyacinths and hydrilla, foreign species that water district officials say would clog the channels if left unchecked. But some sportsmen say the fishing was better when the hyacinths were more abundant, and they worry about the long-term effects of the chemicals.

Conservation efforts have also angered airboaters, who have been banned from the treasured 8,000-acre Flying Eagle Ranch on the Withlacoochee River banks.

Adams, who remembers the river as it was 60 years ago, would prefer that everyone just stay out—government, developers, and industry alike. "Tell them we want the river left alone," he said. "Let it go back to nature. Nature will take care of it." ~

Alafia

by Greg Lamm

LENGTH: 25 miles long from Alderman's Ford, where the Alafia's north and south prongs meet, to Hillsborough Bay.

DRAINAGE AREA: 335 square miles.

ORIGIN OF NAME: Alafia is pronounced "AL-a-fi" or "al-a-FI-a," depending on which person is quizzed. Another point of contention is the origin of the name. *Alafia* in Spanish means oleander, which blooms on the river bank, but some historians say the word is Indian and means "good hunting ground." Still others contend the name is from "all-a-fire," a description of illumination on the river waters at night caused by a high level of phosphorus.

TYPE: Blackwater, attributed to high concentrations of tannins and organic acids from surrounding swamps and pine forests.

CITIES ALONG THE RIVER: Gibsonton, a community near the junction of the Alafia River and Hillsborough Bay, and Riverview, upriver east of U.S. 30l.

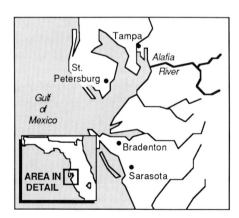

SIGNIFICANCE: Once a paradise for fishermen and hunters, the Alafia River in recent decades has lost its fishing and recreational significance because of voluminous pollution. Nearby phosphate mining has degraded the Alafia into an industrial stream, but state agencies and private preservation groups are struggling to re-establish the river as a natural attraction by enforcing restrictive regulations against continuing discharge of waste water into the river.

Norma Caldwell doesn't need a biological study to tell her something has gone afoul in the Alafia River. A small but sturdy woman, she has spent most of her 76 years living a hard and often colorful life on this river that meanders west from headwaters in Polk County through Hillsborough County into Hillsborough Bay.

Her wood-frame house, located on river property shared by her relatives, is one of the few signs of the old river life. It sits among oaks and pines, sheltered from a world of new subdivisions and freeways nearby. Inside the dark house, the pungent, spicy smell of nasturtiums keeps the insects away. Fixtures for gas lanterns remain on the walls. Doors and windows stick, and the floor is not level, victim of a mighty oak growing too near the roof, Caldwell explained.

There was a time when mullet would leap into boats, Caldwell recalled, when the Florida panther lurked in river woods, when early river settlers shot alligators by the score to protect families and livestock. But today is a time of environmental struggle. Blame it on development, a century of phosphate mining and processing, on the dumping of garbage and sewage into the river and its arteries. "I don't like it," Caldwell said of pollution and development along the river. "They're just wrecking things."

There is hope, though, that the river will be saved. State officials, citing the river's poor water quality, disqualified the Alafia in 1987 from a protective designation as an "Outstanding Florida Water." But because the Alafia flows to the bay, the river has been included in a Tampa Bay restoration project funded by the state legislature.

Hillsborough County government officials hope to have the Alafia designated as a state scenic river and thus limit development along its banks in some areas. The county also would like to purchase and preserve about 850 acres of environmentally sensitive land on or near the river. The parcels include more than 200 acres near Lithia Springs, a popular swimming and camping park owned by Gardinier, Inc., which pumps water from the spring for its nearby fertilizer operation.

"We've been trying to get people interested in doing something about the Alafia for some time," said Douglas Farrell, chief biologist in the state Department of Environmental Regulation's Tampa office. But, he pointed out, the state doesn't even have enough staff and money to follow up on Alafia River studies conducted in 1983 and 1984.

One such study concluded the Alafia's north prong was one of the most environmentally stressed river systems in this part of Florida. Another showed high levels of coliform, a bacteria from sewage dumping that can cause diseases. That study was sent to Tallahassee and used to set DER standards for sewage discharge, Farrell said. However, little in the way of actually cleaning up the Alafia has trickled back. "It's a mess, if you want to know the truth about it," said Farrell. "And I don't see it getting any better."

If its channel cut a straight path, the Alafia and its north prong would extend about 30 miles from west of Bartow through the heart of Florida's mining country and to the bay. The south prong of the Alafia River originates in southern Polk County. It bends north to meet the north prong at Alderman Ford near Lithia and the State Road 39 Bridge in Hillsborough County. More than 20 other smaller creeks or branches also feed the river. Because of its rocky bottom, which turns several bends into churning shoals during dry periods, the Alafia is not safe for motorboats east of Bell Shoals. But the upriver area, with its patches of unspoiled flatwoods and park lands, is popular for canoeing and camping.

Through the years, the lore of the Alafia has been spiced with tales of buried treasure and outer space encounters, passed on and added to by the hearty people who have lived on or near its banks. The Alafia River has a history with native Indians that predates biblical times, according to local historians who have studied huge mounds of oyster and clam shells. But the more recent history of whites along the river is far more destructive.

In 1848, settler James Alderman cut down the dense forest on the steep banks of the Alafia, allowing horses and wagons to ford the south end of the river and opening the area to development. By 1902, before the age of radio and television, Alderman's Ford became popular with politicians who would stage picnic rallies there. Communities such as Riverview, Peru, and Magnolia had already sprung up along the river and its prongs in the late 1800s when one of the world's largest phosphate deposits was discovered upstream in the Bone Valley area. The area is still an important source of phosphate, although it rapidly is being depleted, according to industry officials. Phosphate is used in fertilizers, manufacturing, and food-processing industries.

In 1955, the Florida State Board of Health called phosphate industry discharges "the single greatest threat on healthy biological conditions on the Alafia River." Six years later, state scientists classified the Alafia an "industrial stream" because they said the river waters were unsuitable for most uses. But according to Norma Caldwell, there was concern for the health of the river even before then.

In the early 1900s, river folks who re-

Alafia

Below: With headwaters in both Polk and Hillsborough counties, the Alafia is fed by 20 small creeks and springs before it empties into Hillsborough Bay.

Bottom left: Waters of the Alafia once were as pure as the springs that fed it, but pollution from phosphate plants along its shores have sullied it into an "industrial" river.

Bottom right: A trio of turtles survive the polluted river, which state agencies and environmentalists are trying to restore to its once pristine condition.

Alafia   79

membered the crystal-clear waters of the Alafia before the age of mining tried to focus attention on the pollution, Caldwell said. A Hillsborough County commissioner at the time, W. T. Williams, even convinced several officials from Washington, D.C., to come to Florida for a firsthand look. But the miners had one up on Williams, beating his welcoming party to the Tampa train station, then whisking the Washington officials off for a wining-and-dining session. "They went back to Washington saying there was no need to do anything for those poor crackers," Caldwell said.

Until recent decades, it was common practice to discharge into the Alafia waste water used to separate the phosphate from sand and clay. At the same time, heavy rains, causing flooding, washed by-products of mining and phosphate processing into nearby streams and rivers. In the early 1970s, for example, a major spill occurred at the Sydney Mine operation upstream. The spill turned the water the color of café au lait, according to one old-timer. It sent river residents out in boats with rakes and pitchforks to remove dead snook up to three feet long, said Martha Kjeer, a member of the Alafia River Basin Board and of Citizens for Alafia River Preservation. "It literally killed every fish in the river," Kjeer said.

Today, because of public pressure, the mining industry is more sensitive to the environment. Since environmental restrictions on the industry were strengthened in the mid-1970s, experts say the river has shown signs of recovering. Manatees and otters still frequent the river's mouth at Hillsborough Bay. Fishermen still talk of catfish catches upstream as they wade in the shallows among towering cypress trees and the humbled cypress stumps.

But serious problems remain. In 1987 heavy rains flooded grounds surrounding the Gardinier phosphate plant near Gibsonton and the mouth of the Alafia, forcing the company to deliberately dump 14 million gallons of acidic waste. The spill caused another fish kill and poisoned nearby shellfish beds. After the spill, the company expanded on-site rentention areas and paid a $200,000 fine to the state Department of Environmental Regulation.

In 1988, county commissioners gave IMC Fertilizer, Inc., permission to expand its Kings-

ford Mine near the Alafia River by about 3,000 acres. The mining, slated to begin in 1992, has raised new questions about possible adverse effects on the river.

But mining industries do not bear the entire blame for the Alafia's woes. For years, governments and developers have discharged sewage into the Alafia and connecting streams.

Runoff from the nearby cattle pastures that dot the river bank also spills into the Alafia. The sewage and runoff problems are blamed for making the water in some areas unfit for swimming. Signs posted at Lithia Springs Park, for example, warn bathers not to venture out into the river waters because of pollution.

Environmental officials know that if they are going to improve the quality of Tampa Bay, they must do something about the bad water coming from the Alafia and other tributaries, said Michael Perry of the Southwest Florida Water Management District. According to Perry, 80 percent of Tampa Bay's pollution comes from rivers or storm-water runoff. Officials are currently working on a strategy to address how to clean up the bay and rivers and where to start. Perry said it will be the 1990s before people notice an improvement in the Alafia. "What we're concerned about is not putting a Band-Aid on the problem," he said.

Of course, to folks like Caldwell, whatever is done will not bring back the Alafia as they remember it. New nearby roads now upstage the river itself as the area's major means of transportation. Caldwell recalls that "the first post office in Riverview didn't even have a parking lot. It had a boat dock."

As she spoke, an Air Force jet invaded the quiet afternoon on the river. And nearby, cars and trucks zoom over a bridge crossing the river. During the day, Caldwell said, the traffic cannot be heard, but at night the road noise sometimes keeps her awake. "The river amplifies the sounds," she said. "Sometimes it's just ceaseless."

There was a time that when folks talked about the Alafia River they did not talk about pollution. They talked about treasure and space travelers. Some still do.

One treasure tale involves a Civil War military payroll of gold and silver aboard a Confederate ship trying to run a Union blockade of the Alafia. Because the Rebel ship was outnumbered seven to one, so the story goes, the Confederate captain decided to bury the payroll along the river bank. But the Civil War treasure sank deep in the soft mud, and people today are still looking for it.

Treasure seekers also have searched over the years for a pirate's buried treasure, according to a story passed along in *The WPA Guide to Florida*, a Depression-era publication commissioned under President Franklin Roosevelt's New Deal. The guide gives this account: A group of people in the Gibsonton area, aided by an old chart, "unearthed a skeleton sitting upright and below it a metal disk with the points of the compass and a needle marked on its face." In the excitement, a group member snatched up the compass without looking at the direction the needle was pointed. The party searched for days, but no treasure was found.

According to another account of the Alafia in the WPA guide, Bell Shoals is the actual site of futurist Jules Verne's 1865 novel *From the Earth to the Moon*. It is here that a 900-foot cannon to send Verne's adventurers to the moon was supposed to have been cast and erected. In his novel, the launch site was on the eastern banks of the "Alifia [sic] Creek; a little river which flows into Hillsborough Bay twelve miles above town [Tampa]." Early versions of the Verne novel had the space travelers doomed to a never-ending orbit around the moon because the cannon was not aimed properly. Horrified readers objected, so Verne rewrote the finish to bring the nineteenth-century astronauts safely back to earth.

For more than 60 years, Alafia river folks believed a partially buried piece of machinery on the banks was a fragment of the giant make-believe cannon described in the novel. The 10-foot shaft with vines attached to both ends was later unearthed and proved to be part of a gristmill. Verne said the Bell Shoals spot was 1,800 feet above sea level, indicating that he probably culled the description of the site from someone else's imaginative account. Verne, a Frenchman, only visited America once during a week in April 1865. During his visit, the author of *Around the World in 80 Days*, *20,000 Leagues Under the Sea*, and *Journey to the Center of the Earth* never left New York state.

Like many of Verne's works, *From the Earth to the Moon* was later made into a movie. But it was not filmed along the Alafia. ~

Myakka

by Tim Dorsey and Rick Barry

LENGTH: 68 miles, beginning near the Manatee-Hardee county line and ending in the Gulf of Mexico at Port Charlotte.

DRAINAGE AREA: 235 square miles.

ORIGIN OF NAME: *Myakka* is believed to be an Indian generic term meaning "big" or "big water."

TYPE: Blackwater. The water is dark in color as a result of high concentrations of tannins and organic acids that come from surrounding swamps and pine forests.

CITIES ALONG THE RIVER: Myakka City, Warm Mineral Springs, Port Charlotte.

SIGNIFICANCE: The river is used primarily for fishing and recreational purposes, with the Myakka State Park, considered one of the best in the state, being the biggest attraction.

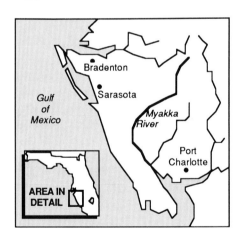

Killer turtles swoop from overhanging trees, the Myakka's river people claim, and a sea monster once lurked in the waters near the pit where José Gaspar buried his doubloons. But beneath the hype and legend, the amber river flows through some of Florida's most treasured wilderness, and through history as real as mastodons, Ponce de Leon, and the Indian and Civil Wars. The river's heritage, a heady mixture of fact, legend, and sometimes comical folklore, provides a backdrop as eclectic as the waterway's geography.

A trip down the Myakka is a solitary, 68-mile journey on a twisting, canopied river through Manatee, Sarasota, and Charlotte counties, where the wildlife is as abundant as its lore. Still, the river is relatively unknown, even within the counties it traverses.

Its importance to the area, however, was not lost on the legislature that in 1985 designated it as Florida's second "Wild and Scenic River," the first being the Loxahatchee in Palm Beach County. That designation aimed to preserve a resource that local fishermen, boaters, naturalists, and historians have valued for generations.

At its headwaters, the Myakka is a narrow brown stream, flowing gently from the Manatee-Hardee county line and snaking to the southwest, soon giving birth to the Upper and Lower Myakka Lakes in Florida's largest state park, which bears the river's name.

In the 1840s, surveyors were told by Indians that the river's name was "Myakka." The name is believed to be an Indian generic term "big" or "big water," which could explain why Lake Okeechobee once went by the same name.

The Manatee County community closest to the river is Myakka City, set back a few hundred yards from its banks near the county's eastern border. Fifty years ago, local politicians campaigning in Myakka City would stump for votes in an oak-shrouded clearing on the river, according to 67-year-old Eddie Durrance, who also recalls horse racing during his childhood along the river. Today, that riverside vista is Crane Park, a small county picnic and fishing area.

Soon after crossing into Sarasota County, the river makes a 12-mile run through Myakka River State Park, a picturesque 29,000-acre preserve where the river forms two large lakes. The park teems with many of the state's native birds, deer, wild boar, alligators, and other wetland animals.

At the south end of the park's lower lake, the river fills a 150-foot deep sinkhole where a limestone bed collapsed. From there, the river's waters are readily navigable by canoe or small outboard as it meanders through long stretches of untouched oak hammocks, palms, and scrubland.

Leaving the park, the river soon widens to 40 feet or more and then to 100 feet as it winds through lower Sarasota County, where rising tides and drought turn the water brackish as far as 20 miles from its mouth. A seven-foot shark was once caught 20 miles upriver.

Fishermen casting for bass, bream, and channel cats from small outboards are likely sights near the 50-year-old Snook Haven fish camp east of Venice. That stretch might well provide the first human encounter of a river journey southward. The fish camp itself is a popular combination restaurant/boat launch just south of Interstate 75's Exit 34 east of Venice. Several country bands have packed outdoor barbecues at the camp most Sundays since the 1960s.

But Snook Haven's T-shirts tout the place not as a rural retreat, but as the "Home of the Killer Turtles." Ask, and manager Andy Huset explains patiently, as if he thought everyone knew by now, that a group of rogue, tree-climbing South American turtles was released in the area during the filming of a movie there in the 1930s. It seems the turtles, which

grow to weigh 40 pounds or more, climb out on the trunks of palms overhanging the river to dive on their prey, including, he claims, the occasional unwary visitor. Hence, Huset insists on personally guiding tourists upriver in a covered pontoon boat in search of the beasts.

"They're a very vicious breed of turtle," Huset said with a straight face. "I had one come through the roof of the tour boat once. It was probably just looking for food, though." Confirmed sightings, he acknowledged, are rare.

It is George Kent, alias "Bear," 36, born no more than 10 miles from Snoop Haven, who shares the tale of the sea monster that he swears boaters and river folks sighted off and on for years during the 1940s, each one describing its two or three huge coils rising and falling in the river's early morning mist. "No kidding, I heard the stories all the time growing up," Kent says. "I went and looked it up in the library. Turned out to be an anaconda that got loose from one of those tourist zoos that were all along the highways back then. But it had people here thinking they were crazy."

According to another legend, the marauding pirate José Gaspar escaped authorities in Charlotte Harbor and fled up the Myakka with a small band of men and a small fortune in gold. When the river became too narrow to navigate, Gaspar buried the gold in Manatee County and killed his crew. Local Indians are supposed to have witnessed the whole affair and passed the details from generation to generation. But the story enters the realm of documented fact in 1913 when groups of local landowners caught gold fever and dug a small crater in a futile search for the rumored loot. The "Myakka Gold Hole" is now a small pond, Sarasota County historian John McCarthy says.

There is very little flow over the last 25 miles or so of the river's run to Charlotte Harbor; tidal pressure virtually cancels any downstream current.

Overall, the water quality over the river's entire course is good, according to studies by the state and Mote Marine Laboratory in Sarasota. Jono Miller is director of New College's environmental studies program and chairman of the 34-member Myakka River Coordi-

Myakka

Left: The Myakka, translated as "big," spreads its fullest in Charlotte County at El Jobean.

Below, left and right: Once it enters the state's largest park, the river expands into two huge lakes whose shorelines continuously rustle to alligators, deer, wild boar and flights of exotic birds.

nating Council. The council, created by the legislature with its "Wild and Scenic River" and "Outstanding Florida Water" designations, is studying the river and devising a management plan for the river's future. Quoting from a Mote study, Miller says pollution was reported "mild to moderate in 1980" and only slightly deteriorated four years later. Slightly higher than acceptable levels of fecal bacteria were blamed on runoff from pastureland upstream.

Development has remained limited over the river's entire length, and except for a few dozen homes, the state park, two campsites, and the restaurant, very little has been built directly on the river. In fact, the river has a track record of reverse development. Remains of 10,000-year-old humans show that prehistoric man lived along its banks. Later, extensive Indian settlements thrived until the 1600s when Spanish explorers virtually wiped them out, either by force or exotic diseases brought from Europe.

Juan Ponce de Leon, searching for the fountain of youth, explored the mouth of the river in Charlotte Harbor. Some historians, including McCarthy, believe the harbor may have rivaled St. Augustine as the country's earliest permanent settlement had de Leon, on a re-

turn trip to the area with settlement in mind, not been mortally wounded by Indians.

In the last half of the nineteenth century, with most of the Indians and Spanish gone, cattle grazed freely on the vast open ranges surrounding the river. These ranches became increasingly important during the Civil War, when Confederate troops needed livestock and farmlands in remote areas that would escape Yankee detection.

Today, the river's run is remote and mostly uninhabited. Even so, the nearby coastal development is too much for some purists.

Engineer Herman White, 38, who has fished the waters of the upper Myakka since he was a toddler, says he moved away from the area two years ago when the cities of Bradenton and Sarasota got too big and the urban sprawl began to move eastward. Today he lives in rural Marianna in the Panhandle.

On a visit back to the area, he and his wife, his mother and father, came straight to the river to fish. They had it to themselves. "I tell you," he said, "if all of Manatee County could have stayed just like this, I'd never have left. I'd spend the rest of my life right here." ~

Waccasassa

by Tom Henry

LENGTH: 29 miles.

DRAINAGE AREA: 610 square miles.

ORIGIN OF NAME: Taken from a Seminole Indian phrase meaning "where there are cows" or "where there is cattle."

TYPE: Blackwater.

SIGNIFICANCE: One of the most undeveloped rivers in Florida, the Waccasassa is a hidden treasure for outdoor enthusiasts. Wildlife ranges from hogs to alligators. About three-quarters of the river is accessible only by canoes and kayaks. There is a good chance the river will be preserved for years to come because the state Department of Natural Resources and the Georgia-Pacific timber company own nearly all of the surrounding land and have expressed no desire to sell.

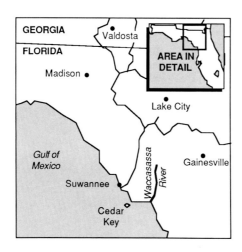

In some areas, it is a river so quiet that its tranquility can be broken by turtles sliding off a rock. Yet only a few miles downstream, where it widens like the mighty Mississippi, the river suddenly becomes a rugged playground for recreational boaters. Alligators and osprey keep watch. Deer dine off the growth along the shore; hogs scarf whatever food they happen to find. Upstream, otters play while catfish and bass try to avoid sports fishermen.

Welcome to the Waccasassa River, a 29-mile glimpse of the way things used to be. Other parts of the state may enjoy growth, but this is one place that seems content to be old Florida. "I would say it's one of the most undiscovered rivers in Florida," said Lawrence Messer, who moved from Gulf Hammock four years ago to run the only marina on the river.

Location and a lack of development have combined to keep the river a secret. The Waccasassa runs through the heart of Levy County, which ranks near the bottom in population density in the state. In the 1980 census, Levy County had 18 people per square mile, the 55th lowest density among Florida's 67 counties. Pinellas County, by comparison, ranked first, with 2,759 people per square mile.

In addition, there are no incorporated cities within miles of the river. Gulf Hammock, a town that thrived during the long-gone lumbering era, is the closest community. It is unincorporated and currently has about 400 residents. The next closest is Otter Creek, which has 200 residents.

A few rustic homes exist along some creeks that feed into the river and its tributaries, but the Waccasassa itself is virtually undeveloped. Nearly all of the land along the river is owned by the state Department of Natural Resources and the Georgia-Pacific timber company. The state plans to preserve its acreage; Georgia-Pacific plans to use its land for timber production and replanting while maintaining a buffer along the river, officials said.

"It's probably one of the more undeveloped areas of the state. I don't think it would ever be sold," said Dewey Weaver, a spokesman for the state's Game and Fresh Water Fish Commission.

Several residents share Weaver's opinion. "In other counties, your Yankees come down and buy up the waterfront property and plop a house down. Here, that's just not going to happen," Messer said.

The lack of development has kept the river one of the cleanest in Florida, officials say. Occasionally, a beer can or two and other types of litter can be found along the shore, but for the most part there is not much evidence that anyone has disturbed the river or the wildlife.

From turkeys to bald eagles, the area is home to an array of creatures, and it is one of the few remaining wildlife habitats adorned with acres of oaks and black gum trees. "Just about every kind of wildlife that exists in Florida lives there, with the exception of the Florida panther," Weaver said.

Even the name suggests wildlife. History books say the name is believed to be a Seminole Indian phrase meaning "where there are cows" or "cattle range." It is derived from the Seminole words *wacca*, which means "cow" or "cattle," and *sasi*, which means "there are."

Gulf Hammock resident Frank Couch, Jr., hoping to generate support for the river and to raise money for the Levy Association for Retarded Citizens, began sponsoring a Wild Hog Canoe Race on the Waccasassa 12 years ago. Canoeists paddle a daring and sometimes tricky 15-mile course from Otter Creek to Gulf Hammock in what is billed as the "biggest, funniest, wildest race in the state." The event has become one of the biggest along the river, attracting more than 100 entrants in re-

cent years from as far away as North Carolina.

Chances are that unless you're an expert canoeist, you won't see much of the Waccasassa River. About 22 miles—three-quarters of its length—is accessible only by canoe. The last seven miles downstream is accessible to motorboats, but there is only one launching site. It is three miles west of U.S. 19, where Levy County has a public boat ramp and Messer's private Waccasassa Fish Camp is located.

Rarely does anyone try to maneuver around that part of the river with anything but a skiff. "Most people around here have cheap canoes or johnboats—just something to get them there and back," Messer explained. "You don't see any of those high-powered boats. If you see a big, nice bass boat, you know he's from Ocala, Gainesville, or Jacksonville."

From bream to trout, the river is stocked with a variety of fish. Redfish, however, are off limits because of a ban on their catches—both by commercial and recreational fishermen—imposed by state and federal governments. But despite the redfish ban, the fish camp continues to draw a core of visitors. And a certain camaraderie exists among those who live near the facility and those who visit it on a regular basis.

There are a dozen or so homes in the woods nearby, with other residents living closer to U.S. 19. Many of the people, even if they live miles apart, have gotten to know each other by name and a bit about the families who use the river. "You can't find any better people. They're just plain ol' cracker people," said Earl Minger, 71, a Gulf Hammock resident who has 40 years of experience on the river.

James "Dug" Cosey, a former truck driver who ran the Waccasassa marina for 13 years before Messer arrived in 1984, put it this way: "You can't say we're a close-knit family, but if somebody has a problem, everybody rushes to help."

Randall Williams, 62, a resident whose father, Johnny Williams, built the fish camp 50 years ago, said the facility became the center of a tiny community of outdoorsmen living in the woods and bound by the river that drew them together. "I don't know what it is about

Waccasassa

Despite the occasional human homesteader, the tranquil Waccasassa River remains a centuries-old domain for eagles, bear, wild hogs, and turkey.

the river," Williams said. "It's just something that attracts people."

Little has been recorded about the Waccasassa's past. Officials with Levy County, the state Department of Natural Resources, the Game and Fresh Water Fish Commission, and the Suwannee River Water Management District admit the information they have about the river is skimpy. But local residents say logs were often floated down the river during lumbering's heyday. And at one point near the mouth of the river, there are remnants of a structure that used to support a train that carried the logs. The train has been dormant for years and is now featured as a display at a rest stop on U.S. 19. Other remnants along the river include a tin shack where local residents sold mullet and an abandoned retreat called Swilley's Hide-Away.

According to a booklet published by the Levy County Archives Committee, a military fort and a military road were located near the river in the mid-1800s. Settlers were said to have sought refuge inside the fort when Indians were on the warpath. The structure, Fort Jennings, was built so that it jutted slightly over the Waccasassa River. Occupants under attack could get water by lowering a bucket attached to a rope.

Legend has it that during one skirmish, a government courier came riding down the old military road with the Army payroll—gold coins in his saddlebags—and retreated when he found Fort Jennings empty. Sensing Indians nearby, he buried the gold near the road, sketched a location map, and ran for his life, but was never seen again. Eighty years later,

after learning of the tale, someone dug holes along the old road in search of the gold, but it is not known whether he was successful.

Another anecdote mentions Stafford's Island, named for a man who lived there as a hermit during the same era. However, possibly because of the man's hermit existence, there is little documentation about the island other than to say it is located in the lower portion of the Waccasassa and has been casually referred to in numerous records of the 1800s.

There also have been discrepancies over how to spell the river's name. Current state and local maps, records, and agencies consistently spell it Waccasassa, but research by the Levy County Archives Committee shows the river was once spelled "Wacassassa." In the 1800s, apparently after seeing handwriting that looked like an *f* for each double *s*, local residents began spelling it "Wacafafa." But the practice was not done consistently enough to catch on, according to the archives committee.

Many people do agree that the future of the Waccasassa looks promising. Though Levy County will be predominantly rural for years to come, the plan to extend Florida's Turnpike from Wildwood in Sumter County to U.S. 19 near the Levy County town of Lebanon Station will probably change the face of the area, residents say.

"I think U.S. 19's going to change a lot, but I don't think the river will," Minger said. "I think it'll pretty much stay the way it is, unless somebody gets hold of this land along the river." ~

Suwannee

by Del Marth

LENGTH: 207 miles in Florida; 280 miles long when including Big Alligator Creek in Georgia, which is a headwater tributary to the Suwannee. The river proper begins in the Okefenokee Swamp, a vast wetland wilderness in southeast Georgia and northeast Florida, and enters the Gulf of Mexico north of Cedar Key.

DRAINAGE AREA: 9,630 square miles.

ORIGIN OF NAME: Thought to be derived from the Indian word *swani*, meaning "echo." Explorer Hernando de Soto, who crossed the Suwannee five miles downstream from Dowling Park, called it "River of Deer."

TYPE: A combination blackwater/spring-fed river. In its upper reaches the water is tannic because it drains a swamp. Downstream, the dark color lessens in intensity as spring discharge becomes a greater part of the flow.

COURSE: From the Okefenokee Swamp the Suwannee flows southward to White Springs, then westward where its valley crosses a bed of hard clay. About 25 miles farther downstream the river returns to its southward course to the Gulf.

DEPTH: Generally more than seven feet from tidewater upstream to Ellaville, except for scattered shoals. The channel at the mouth is dredged to prevent shoaling. Upstream from Ellaville the depth may be as great as six feet but is one foot or less over shoals during dry periods.

MAJOR TRIBUTARIES: In Florida, the Santa Fe River is the major tributary. In Georgia, tributaries are the Withlacoochee and Alapaha rivers, which join the Suwannee in Florida.

CITIES ALONG THE RIVER: The largest town bordering the Suwannee is White Springs, population 781.

SIGNIFICANCE: Chiefly recreational boating, fishing, and swimming. Agriculture along its shores include field crops such as melons, tobacco, peanuts, and corn. Industry is limited to phosphate mining and timber growing.

The water flows with a mesmerizing slowness, shaded from the searing summer sun by parasols of oak tree limbs laden with moss. Sometimes, around the bend, tourists softly paddling a canoe can be heard singing "Way Down Upon the Swanee River." All the world, it seems, has heard about the Suwannee River. Fortunately, only a few people court her.

Not because of her breeding, which certainly is suspect. She was, after all, beget in the bowels of the simmering Okefenokee Swamp, across the state line in Georgia. And not because of her beauty, which certainly is sumptuous once she leaves her birthplace and matures down a 207-mile meander through

Florida. But because a coterie of chaperones has jealously protected her. Nearly every environmental organization in the United States, from the Audubon Society to the Sierra Club, keeps their eyes on the Suwannee River.

"We don't have all the state controls," said Jane Walker of the Florida Defenders of the Environment, "but we're optimistic about the river's future, mainly because of the new SWIM [Surface Water Improvement and Management] law. Its money will be used to keep track of any river pollution problems, and to manage it properly so as to maintain the condition of this wonderful resource."

All who live near the Suwannee, and even those who do not, covet the river's unsullied complexion. "It is one of the last great rivers existing in its natural state," says Dave Morine of the Nature Conservancy. A private, nonprofit conservation group headquartered in Virginia, the conservancy buys environmentally endangered lands.

So dear to many is the Suwannee, in fact, that its most constant consort, the Suwannee River Water Management District, has in five short years purchased 17,630 acres on the river at a cost of $11 million. The acquisitions have made the people of Florida the largest landholder on the Suwannee. And in the next nine years, the district plans to spend millions more for another 52,000 acres. "The mission is not restoration, but preservation," says Dennis Murrin of the Department of Environmental Regulation. "Unlike most Florida rivers, the Suwannee is in good shape." A virtuous Southern belle, in reality.

She has had her suitors, of course. Most persistent has been the Occidental Chemical Company at Jasper. Owned by Armand Hammer, it began mining phosphate in 1965 on 75,000 acres along the Suwannee. But, because "Oxy" regularly monitors its discharges into adjacent waters and has restored land that it has mined, some generous environmentalists consider the corporation a responsible neighbor.

No one was that complimentary to the city dandy who showed up in 1987 with a plan to build 4,000 campsites, called the Suwannee Trails Camp Resort, directly on the river's banks. He was Robert W. Browning of Palatka, who foresaw his campground at-

tracting 10,000 people to its 1,300 acres along the Suwannee in Hamilton County. A blitz of protests by environmentalists and state leaders forced Browning to withdraw his plans, despite his emotional plea the venture be approved so "city kids can have the chance to get up in the early morning and see deer grazing." That remark prompted an old-timer to quip: "I wanna meet the wild deer that'll stay put with 10,000 people wanderin' round."

For that matter, also not staying put would be the 42 other types of mammals, the 54 fish species, the 39 kinds of amphibians, and the 232 varieties of birds that hang on to the skirts of the Suwannee as she sashays her way to the Gulf through the counties of Columbia, Dixie, Gilchrist, Hamilton, Lafayette, Levy, Madison, and Suwannee.

The fact of the matter is, environmentalists say, the fauna stays put because people along the river are few and far between. No cities, only towns, sidle up to its banks. The largest is White Springs, population 781, site of a 215-acre park memorializing ante-bellum songwriter Stephen C. Foster, who immortalized the river in his "Old Folks at Home," Florida's official state song.

"Development has been slow along the river," explains Murrin, "because most of the riverfront tracts are large, owned either by paper corporations or farming families." No small factor, too, is the Suwannee's rebelliousness every spring. It floods, quickly and dramatically. "In two weeks the river's water level will rise 20 feet above normal," Murrin says. At those times, access to cabins or second home A-frames is only by boat. Such gorging also interrupts the modest commercial fishing near the river's delta around Hog Island north of Cedar Key, although the Suwannee opens its mouth the widest at this point, nearly 1,000 feet.

Yet, even when not flooding, the Suwannee reveals startling statistics. Her insatiable appetite accepts water from countless tributaries along its route, including such eminently large rivers as the North Withlacoochee and the Santa Fe. In all, the Suwannee drains 9,630 square miles, a drainage area second only to that of the Apalachicola River in the Panhandle. At each day's

Suwannee

Above: A morning fog shrouds the immortalized Suwannee as she prepares for another day's journey from her origin in the Okefenokee Swamp more than 200 miles to her demise in the Gulf of Mexico.

Left: Signs approaching the Suwannee often prompt motorists to sing a few bars of the song that made the river famous.

end, she has contributed 11 billion gallons of spring-fed blackwater to the Gulf of Mexico. Cumulatively, this makes for a staggering figure when computing the age of the river. For geologists contend the Suwannee dates back to the Pleistocene epoch, when it may have been a seaway between archipelago Florida and the mainland.

In the post-mammoth era, Timucuan and Apalachee Indians, the state's earliest residents, used the Suwannee as a neutral battleground that separated their rival camps. Years later, in another war, the antagonists on the river were the Confederates and Union troops, each trying to prevent commercial trafficking on the normally docile waterway. The Grays ran cotton and tobacco and naval stores from one end to the other; the Blues hid along the route trying to sink the South's wood-burning stern-wheelers.

Ever since, fortunately, the demeanor along the Suwannee has been tranquil. Determined to record still another century of undisturbed bliss, state agencies, through protective regulations, are positioning themselves against further trespassing.

Browning's campground version of a Levittown, for example, foundered in part in a maze of government regulations designed to shield the Suwannee from what environmentalists consider a crass and opportunistic suitor. "But, to some extent, the river's development is inevitable," says Donald O. Morgan, executive director of the Suwannee water management district. And, like Walker's Defenders of the Environment, his agency is not so much against development as it is against degradation of the famous waterway.

Should development come, it will be not so much in the upper river north of White Springs, where the Suwannee sometimes measures only 20 feet across. Nor farther north near Big Shoals, where the Suwannee's bouldered bottom pierces the surface, creating an uncharacteristic whitewater rapids. Instead, state planners predict, development is most likely along the lower Suwannee, from Branford southwest through the Manatee Springs State Park region. There, Murrin pointed out, bluffs along the bank can soar 15 feet or more, often out of flood range, making ideal homesites.

In truth, subdivisions along the riverfront have existed since Florida's boom days of the 1920s. But they were few, less than 10. By the 1980s, however, before environmental regulation permeated state statutes, the number had reached more than 300. Living in them primarily are retirees, relatively nonpolluting river denizens who cozy up to the river for the scenery, the leisure, and the occasional home-caught catfish dinner. It is this "esthetic image, and the recreational, that are the primary value of the Suwannee," said Murrin.

Enhancing that image are more than 55 crystalline springs along the Suwannee. Below the surface, the springs gurgle upward from mammoth Floridan Aquifer from which much of the state drinks its water; on the surface, the springs serve as serene spas for swimmers and divers.

In all—the river, the springs, the oaks—it is an intoxicating panorama. To the laziest mind, the placid Suwannee understandably has been described as "the dullest river that I know of." To which Hamp Vartin, who in the 1800s had a plantation on the Suwannee near Branford, was reported to have countered: "Yes, and that is what I like about it. It is quiet and peaceful. It doesn't live a life of strife, like man does." ~

Other Significant Waterways

~~~~~~

Rivers are so abundant in Florida that many are familiar only to residents who live near them. But their distance from urban centers does not diminish their significance or their value as a vital resource to the state. Many of these rivers are in the Panhandle, while others frame the corners of the state. Their names may be familiar but many Floridians would be hard put to drive to them without a road map. Among these waterways are:

Blackwater River — Flowing through hilly forests from south Georgia, the Blackwater enters Florida in Okaloosa County and meanders 49 miles, mostly through neighboring Santa Rosa County, before emptying into Blackwater Bay. Despite its name, the river's waters range from dark to pristine clarity. Appealing features are its sandy white beaches and the Blackwater State Park. Santa Rosa County's seat, Milton, is situated on this scenic river and for years could be reached only by river schooner or stagecoach.

Chipola River — Traversing three Panhandle counties—Jackson, Calhoun, and Gulf, the 89-mile spring-fed Chipola is a cherished portion of the state's canoe trail system. The meandering river flows virtually uninterrupted by development toward Dead Lake, the site of Chipola Park and Dead Lake State Recreation Area. From this point it journeys south, where it eventually blends with the mighty Apalachicola and courses to the Gulf of Mexico.

Choctawhatchee — Often described as one of the South's most beautiful wild rivers, the Choctawhatchee flows past such colorfully named swamps as Dismal and Buzzards Roost. Originating in Georgia, the river runs for 100 miles in Florida, coursing through Holmes County and demarcating the boundary between Washington and Walton counties. Its alluvial waters flow into Choctawhatchee Bay.

Escambia River — An alluvial river that forms the boundary between Escambia and Santa Rosa counties, the 54-mile Escambia is a contortion of bends and oxbows. It also is a fishing paradise before it spills into the marshes at Escambia Bay near Pensacola. The origin of its name is unknown but is believed to be the name given by the Spanish to an area Indian village called San Cosmo y San Damian de Scambe.

Ochlockonee River — Like most Panhandle rivers, the Ochlockonee enters Florida from Georgia where it was born in wetlands. Its Indian name means "yellow water." An alluvial stream 102 miles long, the Ochlockonee separates Gadsden County from Leon County, and Liberty County from Wakulla County. It is a river of many moods and varied scenic wonders, ranging from high pine bluffs to numerous animal habitats, as it flows through the Apalachicola National Forest before emptying into the Gulf. River levels can vary drastically as water is stored or released from Lake Talquin Dam.

Oklawaha River — A central Florida tributary of the St. Johns River, the Oklawaha is a 79-mile blackwater and spring-fed river that runs through Marion County where it lingers near the Ocala National Forest. Farther south it enters Lake County, where it feeds into Lake Griffin and disappears. It is a first-rate fishing river between the Delks Bluff Bridge and the Eureka Dam. Like the north Withlacoochee and the St. Johns, the Oklawaha River was to be dammed and locked as part of the now aborted Cross-Florida Barge Canal.

Perdido River — Although its Spanish name means "lost," the Perdido is quite evident as the major boundary between Florida and Alabama. A blackwater river, it is one of the least known waterways to most Floridians, but its 58-mile course is laden with history dating back to pre-Civil War Days when a ferry was established on it as part of a stagecoach route between Pensacola and Mobile.

St. Marys River — This river originates in the Okefenokee Swamp and forms the boundary between Georgia and Florida at this state's most northeasterly point. The St. Marys runs 127 miles through Florida, weaving around Baker and Nassau counties on its way to an Atlantic Ocean estuary. A 63-mile canoe trail begins in Baker County and ends on the Georiga side of the river.

Santa Fe River — A spring-fed river, the Santa Fe meanders for 76 miles through north central Florida before emptying into the Suwannee River near Branford. While in O'Leno State Park, the Santa Fe disappears into a sinkhole and flows underground for several miles before resurfacing. This natural land bridge over the underground river was part of an old Spanish trail between St. Augustine and Pensacola, a favorite crossing for pioneer wagons. The Santa Fe forms the northern boundaries of Alachua and Gilchrist counties and is fed by the spectacularly clear Ichetucknee River. The river region was the site of numerous Spanish missions during Florida's early settlement.

Wakulla River — Though only a scant 10 miles long, this spring-fed river is a remote paradise for swimming and diving. In the Panhandle's Wakulla County, the river is fed by one of the world's largest springs, four acres in size. The site is rich in archaeological history. The Wakulla ends its short journey when it merges with the St. Marks River for a final sprint into the Gulf of Mexico. ~

Water of a Special Beauty

Florida's Springs

Sidling up to Florida's many rivers are scores of springs—more than 200 of them. And some are still being discovered. No waters of Florida—neither its rivers nor lakes, the Gulf of Mexico nor the Atlantic Ocean—are of such natural beauty, such clarity, and such consistently moderate temperatures as are the constantly flowing springs.

They are a natural overflow from the state's vast groundwater storage and circulation system, and although they are used to a limited degree as a water source for agriculture and industry, their primary use is recreational.

It is estimated that the state's springs pour forth 11,000 cubic feet of water per second, or about 7 billion gallons per day. Yet their flows do vary from year to year, from season to season, and even from day to day. Affecting their output are variations in rainfall. During periods of light rainfall, spring flow declines, just as it increases during wet periods.

Springs are so numerous in Florida because the state sits on limestone and dolomite, sedimentary rocks deposited in shallow seas at various times during the geologic past. These rocks contain small and large interconnected caverns created by groundwater dissolving away limestone. Most Florida springs emerge from these caverns where the rocks open at the land surface.

Thus, a spring is no more than an over-flow or leakage that makes it to the surface from an underground reservoir. The water quality is often excellent—low in salinity, moderate in hardness, constant in temperature ranging from 68 to 72 degrees, and unusually clear.

Springs are rated by the average quantity of water they discharge. First-magnitude springs, for example, are classified as discharging a minimum 100 cubic feet per second; second-magnitude springs discharge between 10 and 100 cubic feet per second; and third-magnitude springs discharge less than 10 cubic feet per second.

Florida contains at least 27 first-magnitude springs, more than any other state. The largest of these, with a flow ranging from 539 to 1,290 cubic feet per second and an average flow of 823 cubic feet per second, is Silver Springs in Marion County. But geologists note that Wakulla Springs in the Big Bend area of Wakulla County has been known to pour forth at some times the greatest measured flow: 1,870 cubic feet per second. Wakulla does not keep it up, however; its output drops at times to a mere 25 cubic feet per second, giving it the widest flow range of any Florida spring.

The accompanying map shows the sites of 181 of the better known Florida springs. Also shown are the sites of seven "psuedo-springs," all in south Florida. Although referred to locally as springs, psuedo-springs are actu-

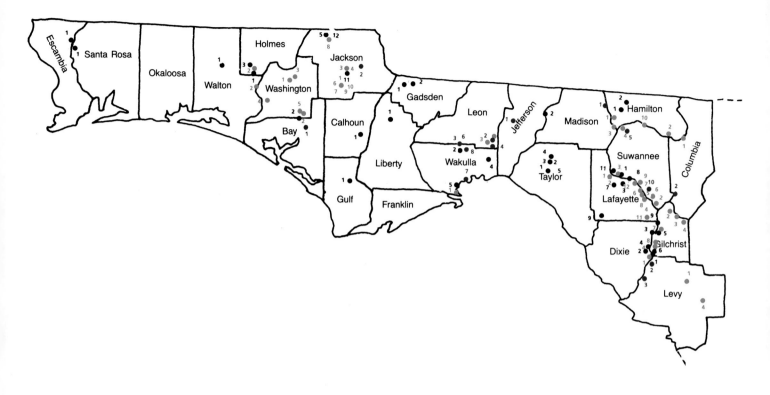

Springs

Explanation

(On map and lists, springs and pseudo springs are numbered serially, by county.)

- ● First magnitude spring: average flow greater than 100 cubic feet per second, 64.6 million gallons per day.

- ● Second magnitude spring: average flow between 10 and 100 cubic feet per second.

- ● Third magnitude spring: spring flow less than 10 cubic feet per second. 6.46 million gallons per day.
- ● Pseudo Spring, flow unknown.

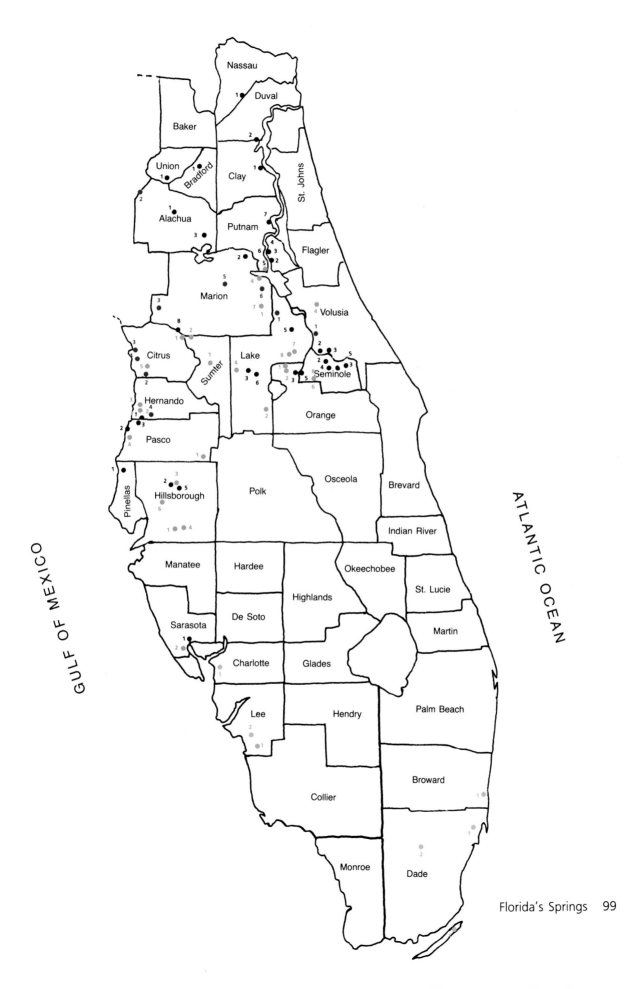

ally outflows from artesian wells often more than 1,000 feet deep.

Springs can be found in 46 of Florida's 67 counties. The major concentration is in the eight counties bordering the Suwannee River. That region has 48 springs, nearly a quarter of the state's total, and almost all of them are near the river.

Florida Springs, by County

*An asterisk denotes a first-magnitude spring.

Alachua County

1. Glen Springs
2. Hornsby Spring*
3. Magnesia Spring
4. Poe Springs

Bay County

1. Gainer Springs*
2. Pitts Spring

Bradford County

1. Heilbronn Spring

Calhoun County

1. Abes Spring

Citrus County

1. Blue Spring
2. Chassahowitska Springs*
3. Crystal River Springs*
4. Homosassa Springs*
5. Ruth Spring

Clay County

1. Green Cove Spring
2. Wadesboro Spring

Columbia County

1. Bell Springs
2. Ichetucknee Springs*

Dixie County

1. Copper Spring
2. Little Copper Spring
3. Guaranto Spring
4. McCrabb Spring

Escambia County

1. Mystic Springs

Gadsden County

1. Chattahoochee Spring
2. Glen Julia Springs

Gilchrist County

1. Bell Springs
2. Blue Springs
3. Ginnie Spring
4. Hart Springs
5. Lumber Camp Springs
6. Otter Springs
7. Rock Bluff Springs
8. Sun Springs
9. Townsend Spring

Gulf County

1. Dalkeith Springs

Hamilton County

1. Alapaha Rise*
2. Holton Spring*
3. Morgans Spring
4. White Springs

Hernando County

1. Bobhill Springs
2. Little Springs
3. Salt Spring
4. Weeki Wachee Spring*

Hillsborough County

1. Buckhorn Spring
2. Eureka Springs
3. Lettuce Lake Spring
4. Lithia Springs
5. Six Mile Creek Spring
6. Sulphur Springs

Holmes County

1. Jackson Spring
2. Ponce de Leon Springs
3. Vortex Blue Spring

Jackson County

1. Black Spring
2. Blue Springs*
3. Blue Hole Spring
4. Bosel Spring
5. Daniel Springs
6. Double Spring
7. Gadsden Spring
8. Hays Spring
9. Mill Pond Spring
10. Springboard Spring
11. Sand Bag Spring
12. Waddells Mill Pond Spring

Jefferson County

1. Wacissa Springs Group*
    Big Spring
    Garner Springs
    Blue Spring
    Buzzard Log Springs
    Minnow Spring
    Cassidy Spring
    Springs No. 1 and 2
    Thomas Spring
    Log Springs
    Allen Spring
    Horsehead Spring

Lafayette County

1. Allen Mill Pond Spring
2. Blue Spring
3. Convict Spring
4. Fletcher Spring
5. Mearson Spring
6. Owens Spring
7. Perry Spring
8. Ruth Spring
9. Steinhatchee Spring
10. Troy Spring*
11. Turtle Spring

Lake County

1. Alexander Springs*
2. Apopka Spring
3. Blue Springs
4. Bugg Spring
5. Camp La No Che Spring
6. Holiday Springs
7. Messant Spring
8. Seminole Springs

Leon County

1. Horn Spring
2. Natural Bridge Spring*
3. Rhodes Springs
4. St. Marks Spring*

Levy County

1. Blue Spring
2. Fannin Springs*
3. Manatee Springs*
4. Wekiva Springs

Liberty County

1. White Springs

Madison County

1. Blue Spring*
2. Pettis Spring
3. Suwanacoochee Spring

Marion County

1. Juniper Springs
2. Orange Spring
3. Rainbow Springs*
4. Salt Springs
5. Silver Springs*
6. Silver Glen Springs*
7. Fern Hammock Springs
8. Wilson Head Spring

Nassau County

1. Su-No-Wa Spring

Orange County

1. Rock Springs
2. Wekiwa Springs
3. Witherington Spring

Pasco County

1. Crystal Springs
2. Horseshoe Spring
3. Magnolia Springs
4. Salt Springs

Pinellas County

1. Health Spring

Putnam County

1. Beacher Springs
2. Mud Spring
3. Nashua Spring
4. Satsuma Spring
5. Forest Spring
6. Welaka Spring
7. Whitewater Springs

Santa Rosa County

1. Chumuckla Springs

Sarasota County

1. Little Salt Springs
2. Warm Mineral Springs

Seminole County

1. Clifton Spring
2. Elder Springs
3. Heath Springs
4. Lake Jessup Spring
5. Miami Springs
6. Palm Springs
7. Sanlando Springs
8. Starbuck Spring

Sumter County

1. Fenney Springs
2. Gum Springs

Suwannee County

1. Bonnet Spring
2. Branford Springs
3. Charles Springs
4. Ellaville Spring
5. Falmouth Spring*
6. Little River Springs
7. Peacock Springs
8. Royal Spring
9. Running Springs
10. Suwannee Springs
11. Thomas Spring
12. Tilford Spring

Taylor County

1. Carlton Spring
2. Ewing Spring
3. Hampton Springs
4. Iron Spring
5. Waldo Springs

Union County

1. Worthington Spring

Volusia County

1. Blue Spring*
2. Gemini Springs
3. Green Springs
4. Ponce de Leon Springs
5. Seminole Spring

Wakulla County

1. Crays Rise
2. Indian Springs
3. Kini Spring*
4. Newport Springs
5. Panacea Mineral Springs
6. River Sink Spring*
7. Spring Creek Springs*
8. Wakulla Springs*

Walton County

1. Euchee Springs
2. Morrison Spring

Washington County

1. Beckton Springs
2. Blue Spring
3. Cypress Spring
4. Blue Springs
5. Williford Spring

Pseudo-springs

Broward County

1. Carlsbad Spa Villas

Charlotte County

1. Hot Springs

Dade County

1. Hurricane Lodge
2. Mineral Springs

Lee County

1. Shangri La Motel Health Resort
2. Warm Springs Spa

Monroe County

1. Pennekamp

Water, Water Everywhere

Florida's Aquifers

If Florida were not already nicknamed the Sunshine State, it could be called the Water State, for the entire peninsula is underlain by underground freshwater reservoirs called aquifers. Six aquifers have been identified in Florida:

— *Floridan Aquifer* measures 82,000 square miles, spreading out beneath all of Florida as well as parts of Alabama, Georgia, and South Carolina. It is so significant that it has been dubbed "Florida's rain barrel." The Floridan lies near the surface of land on the state's Gulf Coast and along the Florida-Alabama border, but sinks to a depth of about 1,700 feet below sea level in the state's westernmost Panhandle region. The average well that taps into the Floridan Aquifer will yield about 1,500 gallons of water per minute. Recharge is by a variety of means according to location. High-recharge areas are cited as the well-drained sand ridges of Orange, Lake, Polk, Pasco, and Hernando counties. Hydrologists have found that rainfall in parts of Hillsborough, Pasco, Hernando, Citrus, and Levy counties soaks directly into the Floridan Aquifer.

— *Sand and Gravel Aquifer* is found under the Panhandle counties of Escambia, Santa Rosa, Okaloosa, and Walton. Maximum well yields from this aquifer are about 2,000 gallons per minute. The aquifer is recharged primarily by rainfall.

— *Biscayne Aquifer* is currently the sole source of potable water for the populous area of southeastern Florida, about 3,200 square miles of Dade, Broward, and Palm Beach counties. The Biscayne is especially susceptible to contamination as it is extremely permeable and dependent on recharge from rainwater.

— *Chokoloskee Aquifer* supplies water to the Big Cypress region of southwestern Florida, as well as to Lee, Collier, and Monroe counties. Recharge to the aquifer comes mainly from rain. Urban development and agricultural use are reducing the fresh water of this underground reservoir and encouraging saltwater intrusion.

— *The Hawthorn Formation and Tampa Limestone aquifers* supply southwestern Florida areas not underlain by the Chokoloskee Aquifer. These water sources are primarily shell beds and limestone and are thought to have no contact with the Floridan Aquifer.

Unnamed groups of smaller aquifers in eastern and southern Florida provide a varying quality of water ranging from excellent to nonpotable. They consist generally of sand and shell deposits that may lie at the land surface.

Florida's rivers play an important role in the state's water system as they collect rainfall and deliver that fresh water to underground aquifers via sinkholes or other porous openings. The Peace River, for example, is estimated to lose between 45 and 53 percent of its flow to a complex of sinkholes that funnel directly to the Floridan Aquifer.

Salt water also underlies Florida, in a layer underneath the freshwater supplies. Found closest to the land surface in coastal areas, salt water is generally held back from water supplies by the pressure of the fresh water and because salt water is heavier and denser than fresh water. That balance is easily upset, however, by human consumption of freshwater supplies. Hydrologists explain that as the "head," or level, of fresh water is lowered, the salt water encroaches. Practices such as pumping from overly deep wells or from wells along the coastlines are inviting saltwater intrusion.

The intrusion problem began during the 1930s and 1940s in southeastern counties such as Dade and Broward. And today, as the demand for water increases with development, saltwater intrusion is increasingly being reported in other regions such as Duval, Flagler, Glades, Hendry, Hillsborough, Lee, Manatee, Martin, Nassau, and Sarasota counties. ~

Guardians of the Rivers

Florida's Water Management Districts

Managing the quality of Florida's rivers, even how water from the rivers may be used, is the job of the state's five water management districts. Each district is responsible for the streams in its region of the state.

Since the creation of the districts in 1972 by the Water Resources Act, their roles have been expanded so that today they are at the forefront of preserving Florida's water resources. Their overall mission is to ensure the preservation, conservation, and appropriate public uses of the rivers. They do so by enacting regulatory programs, acquiring land, promoting public awareness of the rivers, making sure the public's water needs are met, controlling the withdrawal or diversion of water from the rivers, setting standards aimed at reducing flood damage, and even by regulating the location and construction of wells.

To support itself, each water management district is permitted to levy an ad valorem tax within its region. But the districts' greatest income, raised to buy lands for the public along the rivers, comes from a percentage of the state's documentary stamp tax, a levy imposed on all real estate transactions in Florida.

In 1981 Governor Bob Graham created the unique "Save Our Rivers" program, which calls for giving a portion of the documentary tax money to the water management districts. Between 1981 and 1988, the five districts received and spent $200 million of "Save Our Rivers" money to protect Florida's natural waterways, wetlands, and drinking water. The money was used to buy 313,590 acres of land. In the case of the Suwannee River Water Management District, for example, the district has acquired tens of thousands of acres along the famous Suwannee River, making the public the largest landowner of Suwannee riverfront land.

During those eight years, the Northwest Florida Water Management District purchased 88,705 acres at a cost of $23.9 million; the Suwannee River Water Management District purchased 24,500 acres for $11.2 million; the Southwest Florida Water Management District purchased 33,041 acres for $31.5 million; the South Florida Water Management District purchased 110,000 acres for $68.6 million; and the St. Johns River Water Management District purchased 57,344 acres at a cost of $64.1 million.

To expand the districts' role, the legislature in 1987 enacted the Surface Water Improvement and Management Act, or SWIM. Its thrust is to assure restoration of water quality in Florida's rivers and lakes that have become degraded over the years, as well as to preserve the quality of those waterways still in near-pristine condition. SWIM calls for cooperative preservation and restoration programs between state and regional agencies and local governments, all to be implemented by the region's water management district.

The five districts and the counties they cover are as follows:

Northwest Florida Water Management District—Bay, Calhoun, Escambia, Franklin, Gadsden, Gulf, Holmes, Jackson, part of Jefferson, Leon, Liberty, Okaloosa, Santa Rosa, Wakulla, Walton, and Washington.

Suwannee River Water Management District—part of Alachua, part of Bradford, part of Baker, Columbia, Dixie, Gilchrist, Hamilton, part of Jefferson, Lafayette, part of Levy, Madison, part of Putnam, Taylor, Suwannee, and Union.

Southwest Florida Water Management District—Citrus, part of Charlotte, De Soto, Hardee, Hernando, part of Highlands, Hillsborough, part of Lake, part of Levy, Manatee, part of Marion, Pasco, Pinellas, part of Polk, Sarasota, and Sumter.

South Florida Water Management District—Broward, part of Charlotte, Collier, Dade, Glades, Hendry, part of Highlands, Lee, Martin, Monroe, part of Okeechobee, part of Orange, Osceola, Palm Beach, part of Polk, and St. Lucie.

St. Johns River Water Management District—part of Alachua, part of Baker, part of Bradford, Brevard, Clay, Duval, Flagler, Indian River, part of Lake, part of Marion, Nassau, part of Polk, part of Putnam, part of Osceola, part of Okeechobee, part of Orange, St. Johns, Seminole, and Volusia. ~

Outstanding Florida Waters

Worthy of Special Protection

In the late 1970s Florida lawmakers noted that some state waterways were worthy of special protection because of their natural attributes. So they empowered the Department of Environmental Regulation to establish rules that would provide for a special category of water bodies to be referred to as "Outstanding Florida Waters."

To be so singled out, the rules state, a waterway "must be of exceptional recreational or ecological significance." And the "environmental, social, and economic benefits" of so designating a waterway must "outweigh the environmental, social, and economic costs." Once a waterway receives this honored and protective title, no one is permitted to lower its existing water qualilty nor to discharge any materials into it that would significantly degrade it.

Even permits for dredging and filling the cited waterway would have to be in the public's interest. That is, dredge-and-fill permits may not adversely affect public health and safety, interfere with the conservation of fish and wildlife, impede navigation, cause erosion or shoaling, harm the waterway's fishing or recreational value, or disturb historical or archaeological resources.

As of 1988, the Department of Environmental Regulation has labeled 27 bodies of water as special and deserving the "Outstanding Florida Waters" title. They are:

Apalachicola River
Aucilla River
Blackwater River
Butler Chain of Lakes
Chipola River
Choctawhatchee River
Clermont Chain of Lakes
Crooked Lake
Crystal River
Florida Keys
Lemon Bay Estuarine System
Litte Manatee River
Lochloosa Lake
Myakka River
Ochlockonee River
Orange Lake, the River Styx, and Cross Creek
Perdido River
Rainbow River
St. Marks River
Sante Fe River System
Sarasota Bay Estuarine System
Shoal River
Silver River
Suwannee River
Wacissa River
Wakulla River
Wekiva River ~

Paddling through theWilderness

Florida's Canoe Trails

Anear-perfect way to discover and explore Florida's rivers and creeks is by canoe. With that in mind, the state in 1979 passed the Florida Recreational Trails Act, authorizing the establishment of a network of recreational, scenic, and historic trails.

The network is a system of trails intended to encourage not only canoeing but also bicyling, hiking, horseback riding, and jogging through the state's unique wilderness. To be enjoyed along the trails are related activities such as bird watching, photography, picnicking, and fishing.

This statewide network includes 36 canoe trails that were officially designated by the Department of Natural Resources so that people could learn about some of the more than 1,700 rivers and creeks that meander through Florida. These trails cover nearly 950 miles of scenic waterways. They are spread throughout Florida, from the eastern Panhandle area around Pensacola to the southwestern Gulf Coast and the Everglades.

Each canoe trail is a publicly owned stream, though often flowing through private property on each side. In most cases these privately owned river banks are not open to public use. But the waters are public, and therefore available for many recreational uses besides canoeing.

Over the years, the Department of Natural Resources intends to improve and add to the state's canoe trails. For the time being, however, Floridians can enjoy the 36 invitingly pristine trails already established.

The trails are listed with a number and a letter in parentheses after each one. The number is the length of the trail in miles. The letter E stands for "easy," meaning generally flat water with few obstructions and requiring basic paddling skills; *M* stands for "moderate," indicating the trail has some obstructions and sharp turns, a possible strong current, and a need for advanced paddling skills; *S* is for "strenuous," meaning that the trail is difficult in places and should be taken only by experienced canoeists.

1. *Perdido River*. The river forms the boundary between Florida and Alabama, curving through woodlands of pine, cypress and juniper. Small ponds and sloughs hidden along the banks provide canoeing side-trips.

2. *Coldwater Creek*. Along the banks of this Panhandle creek are sandbars perfect for picnicking and camping. The stream itself is crystal clear with a white sand bottom.

3. *Sweetwater/Juniper Creeks*. In Santa Rosa County not far from the Alabama line

Canoe Trails

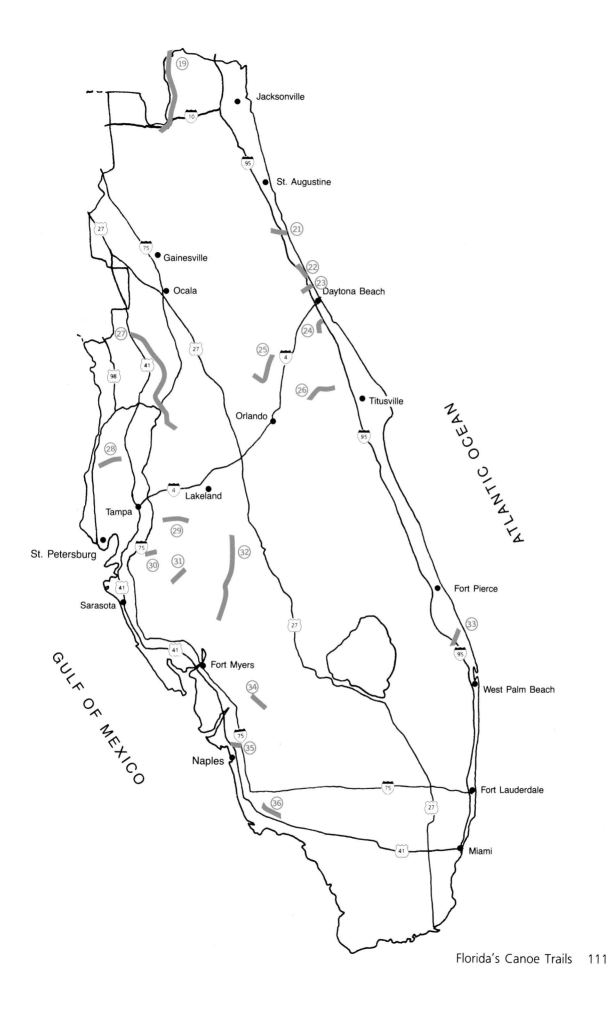

is Sweetwater Creek, a narrow and swift waterway that mellows only after it joins Juniper Creek.

4. *Blackwater River.* This is a fast-flowing river, lined with cedar, maple, and cypress. The canoe trail on this waterway ends at the Blackwater River State Park.

5. *Yellow River.* Framing this stream are hardwood forests and high sandy banks. In its upper portion, the stream is fast-flowing, but downstream, where it deepens, the current is more lethargic. Part of the canoe trail borders Eglin Air Force Base.

6. *Shoal River.* A narrow river of high sandy hills and broad sandbars, this is one of the Panhandle's most scenic canoe routes.

7. *Holmes Creek.* This slow-moving creek winds through verdant swamplands. Punctuated by sharp, twisting bends and low-hanging branches, the canoe trail offers challenges.

8. *Econfina Creek.* Another challenging trail, this one requiring canoeing expertise. The fast-flowing spring water of this creek has cut deep canyons in the limestone.

9. *Chipola River.* Some sections of this trail are for expert canoeists only. The trail begins at Florida Caverns State Park, passing through swamps and forests and rapids. A portion of the trail is designated for the less experienced paddler.

10. *Upper Ochlockonee River.* Low water requires some portaging along this narrow stream, which begins near the Georgia line and heads toward Lake Talquin.

11. *Lower Ochlockonee River.* Winding through Apalachicola National Park, this canoe trail passes high pine bluffs and ends at the Ochlockonee River State Park. The river's level is controlled by Jackson Bluff Dam.

12. *Sopchoppy River.* This swift-water trail courses through the Apalachicola National Forest. It's best to check with the U.S. Forest Service on water levels along this stream as low levels will require many pull-overs and some wading.

13. *Wakulla River.* A slow current and a short trail make a round trip easy along this remote waterway.

14. *Wacissa River.* This narrow, twisting trail runs through the Aucilla Wildlife Management Area.

15. *Aucilla River.* Rapids and manmade dams along this canoe trail mark it for experienced canoeists only.

16. *North Withlacoochee River.* The trail flows through swamplands, past sandy beaches, and across several shoal areas, ending at the Suwannee River State Park.

17. *Upper Suwannee River.* Numerous access points offer a choice of one-day excursions. Accessible from the trail are both the Stephen Foster State Folk Culture Center and the Suwannee River State Park. All canoeists are urged to portage "Big Shoal" rapids on this trail.

18. *Lower Suwannee River.* This is a popular trail because of the abundant wildlife and beautiful scenery along the river. The trail begins at the Suwannee River State Park.

19. *St. Marys River.* Forming the border between Florida and Georgia, this river curves through white sandbars that make scenic camping sites.

20. *Santa Fe River.* This is a good beginner's canoe trail, because of the river's lazy current and gentle curves.

21. *Pellicer Creek.* A short and easy trail, perfect for a half-day canoe trip. Pellicer Creek is south of St. Augustine near the Atlantic Ocean.

22. *Bulow Creek.* Flowing through grassy coastal marshes near the Atlantic Coast, the trail loops around the historic ruins of the Bulow Plantation, continuing on to its terminus at the Intracoastal Waterway.

23. *Tomoka River.* This 13-mile trail begins in the narrows and widens as the river flows through coastal marshes to Tomoka State Park.

24. *Spruce Creek.* Made up of two loops, one a 5-mile trip, the other a 9-mile trip, this trail in Volusia County begins and ends at a landmark called Moody Bridge.

25. *Wekiva River/Rock Springs Run.* Rock Springs Run meets the Wekiva River at the Wekiva Springs State Park, with the trail encompassing both streams before flowing into the St. Johns River.

26. *Econlockhatchee River.* Known as the "Econ," the trail down this stream winds past sandy beaches and oak hammocks. The river is narrow and shallow upstream, broad and deep downstream.

27. *South Withlacoochee River.* This long, 83-mile canoe trail flows out of the Green Swamp and into cypress swamps and pine forests.

28. *Pithlachascotee River.* The short trail down this waterway is laced with tight curves that demand technical paddling, and is recommended only for the experienced canoeist.

29. *Alafia River.* The Alafia flows swiftly over limestone beds, exposing shoals in low water. The trail is only an hour's drive from Tampa.

30. *Little Manatee River.* This trail is a good half-day trip through undisturbed surroundings; the takeout point is the Little Manatee River State Recreation Area.

31. *Manatee River.* The trail is confined to the upper portions of this large river and winds through subtropical vegetation. Water level is controlled by releases from the Lake Manatee Dam.

32. *Peace River.* An ideal canoe trail that meanders peacefully through untouched forests and grassy plains. Opportunities to observe animals, particularly birds, are abundant.

33. *Loxahatchee River.* A variety of wildlife is seen along this waterway, which courses through cypress swamps lush with ferns and orchids. Part of the trail passes through Jonathan Dickinson State Park.

34. *Hickey's Creek.* An easy half-day trip through subtropical hammocks east of Fort Myers. The trail ends at locks on the Caloosahatchee River.

35. *Estero River.* Beginning at Koreshan State Historic Site, the trail heads toward Estero Bay, where canoeists can select a variety of routes to explore mangrove islands before returning upstream.

36. *Blackwater River/Royal Palm Hammock.* This trail loops through Collier-Seminole State Park and is a good choice for beginners. ～

Tranquil Getaways

Florida's State Park System

Many of the state's major rivers and tributaries course through Florida's 105 parks, recreation areas, museum sites, gardens, and preserves, all part of a vast state park system designed to protect and preserve the state's natural resources and cultural heritage. Recreational opportunities are endless, and nearly all the sites can be explored by canoe, boat, or tube.

Most sites (51) are coastal, that is, they border the Atlantic Ocean, the Gulf of Mexico, or adjacent bays and inlets. The Gulf coast harbors the most sites (27), with 18 along the Atlantic and another 6 in the Florida Keys.

Of the state's 105 sites, 34 are classified as recreation areas, 32 as parks, 18 as historical sites, 5 as preserves, 5 as museums, 4 as reserves, 2 as archaeological sites, 1 as a botanical site, and 1 as a geological site. Only one does double duty: Ybor City in Tampa is classified as both a historical site and a museum. Of special interest is an underwater park in the Florida Keys, the John Pennekamp State Park, one of the few sites of living coral reef within the continental United States.

Blessed with more than 1,700 rivers and streams, the state has situated 25 of its parks and recreational and cultural sites along flowing waterways. They are:

Blackwater River State Park—three miles off U.S. 90 northeast of Milton, offering forested campsites and fishing and boating along the Blackwater River.

Blue Spring State Park—on the famous St. Johns River, off Interstate 4 and U.S. 17 two miles west of Orange City, featuring a spring run perfect for swimming.

Crystal River State Archaeological Site—an important pre-Columbian Indian site with artifact exhibits and Indian mounds, west off U.S. 19-98 north of Crystal River.

Florida Caverns State Park—a network of caves three miles north of Marianna through which the Chipola River flows underground.

Fort Clinch State Park—a military site overlooking the Amelia River and abutting the Atlantic Ocean, offering tours presented by park rangers in Union uniforms.

Fort Gadsden State Historic Site—in the Apalachicola National Forest and overlooking the Apalachicola River, a site used as a fort by the British in 1814; on State Road 65 six miles southwest of Sumatra.

Hillsborough River State Park—one of the state's oldest parks and noted for its scenic beauty among hammocks, magnolias, cypress, live oaks, and sabal palms; on U.S. 301 six miles south of Zephyrhills.

Fort Foster—at Hillsborough River State Park, an authentic replica of the fortification built in 1837 during the Second Seminole War to protect the bridge across the river.

Hontoon Island State Park—a 1,600-acre park of cypress swamps and hammocks of cabbage palms, featuring an observation tower viewing the island and waterways; at the St.

Johns River west of De Land on State Road 44.

Ichetucknee Springs State Park—a series of springs that provide one of the most beautiful three-hour tubing runs in all of North America, reached by taking U.S. 27 to Fort White.

Jonathan Dickinson State Park—on U.S. 1 south of Stuart, noted for the scenic Loxahatchee River that courses alongside the park.

Koreshan State Historic Site—on the banks of the Estero River on U.S. 41 south of Fort Myers, a site settled in 1904 by pioneers known as the Koreshan Unity.

Lake Talquin State Recreation Area—a 20,000-acre area including parts of three counties, on a lake backed up by the Ochlockonee River and offering a fabulous picnic site called River Bluff.

Manatee Springs State Park—alongside the famous Suwannee River on one of the major boils of Florida, a first-magnitude spring producing 116 million gallons of crystal-clear water perfect for swimming and boating; six miles west of Chiefland off U.S. 19.

Myakka River State Park—17 miles east of Sarasota on State Road 72, noted for the variety of plant and wildlife abounding along the shores of the twisting Myakka River.

Natural Bridge State Historic Site—setting along the St. Marks River, south of Tallahassee, of the dramatic Civil War battle that left Tallahassee the only Confederate capital east of the Mississippi not captured by the Union.

Ochlockonee River State Park—the Sopchoppy, Ochlockonee, and Dead rivers converge in the park, providing excellent fishing; situated on U.S. 319 south of Sopchoppy.

O'Leno State Park—site of the Santa Fe River, which disappears underground while flowing through the park only to resurface three miles distant, an excellent swimming and picnicking park 20 miles south of Lake City on U.S. 41-441.

San Marcos de Apalache State Historic Site—at the confluence of the St. Marks and Wakulla rivers at the town of St. Marks; arrival point of Spanish explorer Panfilo de Narvaez in 1528 and site of the building and launching of the first ships built by white men in the New World.

Stephen Foster State Folk Culture Center—on the banks of the famed Suwannee River, a 250-acre tribute to the composer, featuring a museum and 200-foot carillon tower; on U.S. 41 at White Springs.

Suwannee River State Park—on the Suwannee and joined by the north Withlacoochee River, offering a panoramic view of the two rivers; situated 14 miles west of Live Oak on U.S. 90.

Three Rivers State Recreation Area—overlooking Lake Seminole, a huge reservoir formed by the merging Flint and Chattahoochee rivers, which pass over Jim Woodruff Dam to become one of Florida's biggest rivers, the Apalachicola; the area is situated off U.S. 90 two miles north of Sneads.

Tomoka State Park—three miles north of Ormond Beach at the confluence of the Halifax and Tomoka rivers; once the site of a Timucuan Indian village.

Torreya State Park—noted for the torreya and Florida yew trees, this park is off State Road 12 between Bristol and Greensboro and overlooks the Apalachicola River from high bluffs cut by deep ravines.

Wekiva Springs State Park—near Apopka off U.S. 441, a beckoning canoe and hiking site fed by a spring that becomes the main source of the Wekiva River, which, after being joined by Rock Springs Run, flows into the St. Johns River 15 miles to the northeast.

The state Recreation and Parks Division charges entrance fees at all sites within the park system: Florida residents are charged $1 per vehicle operator and 50 cents per passenger; the rate is doubled for out-of-state visitors. Florida familes may buy an annual permit for $50, out-of-staters for $80. Individual annual permits are $25 for Floridians, $40 for others.

Fees are also charged for camping. They vary from park to park and from season to season, ranging from $8 to $26 per day. These fees are substantially lower for Floridians who are senior citizens or disabled. Six parks offer vacation cabins, ranging in price from $35 to $100 per day, depending on how many persons occupy a cabin: Gold Head Branch at Keystone Heights, Jonathan Dickinson at Hobe

Sound, Myakka River at Sarasota, Bahia Honda at Big Pine Key, Blue Spring at Orange City, and St. Joseph at Port St. Joe.

All the above fees were in effect in 1989. Each year fees have been raised in an effort to make the state's park system self-sustaining. Because the fees are estimated to produce only half the revenue needed to maintain the park system, further increases are anticipated.

Pets are not allowed in camping areas, on bathing beaches, or in concession facilities, and may be restricted in other designated areas. Where pets are allowed they must be kept on a six-foot leash. ~

Potpourri of Game

Fishing and Hunting

Florida has 37 million acres of woodlands, lakes, and rivers in which to hunt and fish. That has made recreation associated with fishing and hunting a big business in the state. Wildlife experts report that 291 species of fish are found in the waters of the Sunshine State. That includes 115 native freshwater species, plus migratory fishes and exotic fishes. About half of the native freshwater species occur only in the Suwannee River system or west of it. Containing the largest number of these, about 83 species, is the Apalachicola River.

By 1990, it is estimated that fishing licenses sold in Florida will number nearly one million, with about 25 percent of those going to out-of-state residents. Hunting licenses, tags, permits, and stamps will reach a half million, but less than one percent will be purchased by tourists or visitors.

Annual licenses are required both for freshwater and saltwater fishing. They include several types: a license for residents to fish, a combination fishing/hunting license for residents, a nonresident annual license, and a nonresident 10-day license. Residents 65 years of age or older need only a Senior Citizen Hunting and Fishing Certificate, which is available free of charge. A similar free certificate for hunting and fishing is offered to totally and permanently disabled residents. Children under 16 also may fish free, as may military personnel home on leave for 30 days or less. All li-

Keep Hooks Away From Birds

Florida's rivers abound in wild birds, from pelicans to osprey to herons to cranes to the endangered wood stork. Yet each year monofilament fishing lines kill these wild birds when the lines are swallowed or become wrapped around a bird's beak or legs and cause starvation. Fish hooks also have been swallowed, injuring a bird externally or internally. Pelicans, for example, suffer ripped pouches from hooks.

Those fishing Florida's rivers and lakes are urged to prevent hooking water birds by looking before casting a line; never leaving lines unattended as the bird may pursue a catch; not leaving a rod with the line reeled up and the hook dangling; and making every effort to avoid abandoning tangled line in trees and utility lines.

If a hooked or line-tangled bird is found, subdue it by wrapping it in a towel, shirt, or blanket. Be sure to cover its head to further calm it. Beware of the beak, as a frightened bird may strike at its captor. Keep the bird in a cool place and, if possible, take it to a veterinarian or wildlife center.

If no help is available and the bird does not appear critically injured or emaciated, an attempt can be made to carefully remove the line or hook. Hooks are most easily removed if the barb is removed first. No bird should be released with line still tangled around its body.

censes for hunting and fishing can be purchased from the tax collector's office in each county.

Each year the Florida Game and Fresh Water Fish Commission issues a regulations booklet detailing bag limits for various species statewide, as well as special bag limits on certain rivers and lakes. Another booklet issued annually covers hunting regulations, detailing season dates, daily bag limits, season bag limits, open and closed areas for hunting, and legal methods of taking game birds and mammals.

Hunting licenses are issued to both residents and visitors, but a hunter must purchase special additional stamps if he or she wishes to hunt in one of the state's wildlife management areas, or hunt with bow and arrow or with a muzzle-loading gun, or if he or she is hunting waterfowl or turkey. Most hunting in Florida is for white-tailed deer, turkey, bobwhite quail, rabbit, gray squirrel, fox squirrel, and wild hog. Black bear is hunted in restricted areas during a two-month season only.

Nearly all of the state's 62 public wildlife management areas open to hunting are bounded or traversed by one or more of the state's 1,700 rivers and streams. ~

Fouling the Nest

The Impact of Growth and Development

Florida's burgeoning population is placing heavy demands on the state's water systems. Septic tanks, agricultural runoff, storm-water runoff, chemical contamination, surface impoundments, phosphate mining, electric power generating plants, and injection wells are all sources of groundwater contamination.

Septic tanks are still used by about 40 percent of Florida's households to handle about one billion gallons of waste material daily. Although some contamination is always possible with these systems, they are particularly hazardous in wet or poorly draining soils.

Agricultural runoff from materials used in farming or ranching also is a growing hazard. Fertilizers, pesticides, herbicides, and animal wastes easily flow above and below ground to groundwater sources.

Storm-water runoff carries metals such as lead, zinc, and iron into Florida's water sources. Only recently have water management agencies turned their attention to urban storm-water runoff, a source of direct pollution as parking lots, streets, and gutters carry oil, fertilizers, and animal wastes directly into waterways.

Chemical runoff occurs at hundreds of sites in Florida. Petroleum fuels, radioactive materials, explosives, toxic wastes, and pesticides have knowingly or unknowingly been allowed to run into ground and surface water sources. Florida has approximately two dozen highly contaminated dump sites that have great potential for damaging the state's water supply.

Surface impoundments are industrial, municipal, or agricultural sites in which pollutants are collected to be managed. A 1982 study indicated the state had nearly 5,700 surface impoundments, with Hillsborough and Polk Counties accounting for nearly 1,000 of the total. Studies also indicate that current methods of impounding pollutants are inadequate.

Phosphate mining occurs on about 6,000 Florida acres each year. Although reclamation of mined lands has occurred since 1975, disposing of phosphate wastes such as clay takes years under current methods of using settling or so-called slime ponds. Another by-product, gypsum, is radioactive and may be washed into groundwater by rain.

Electric power generating plants produce waste heat that is released into Florida waters. Temperature of plant waste water may be 80 degrees and can raise coastal river temperatures by 5 degrees as low tides pull the warm waters from their source. In winter, the endangered manatee is especially attracted to these warm water sites and some experts worry that if a power generating plant suddenly goes off-line, the basking manatees would be severely affected by the sudden temperature change.

Injection wells are frequently used to inject treated sewage or other unwanted wastes underground. While these injection wells are supposed to place wastes into sites away from drinking water sources, they could contaminate groundwater if improperly constructed or operated. Florida permits waste water from swimming pools, air conditioner returns, and laundry drainage to be injected directly into drinking water aquifers.

Florida's natural water system was designed by nature to be self-cleaning. But with the impact of continuing growth in population and development of new hazardous substances, all that future Floridians may be able to hope for is potable water. ~

Our Dwindling Friends

Florida's Endangered Species

The heightened interest in Florida's environment is reflected in an increased role by the state government in managing natural resources. An example is the state's Game and Fresh Water Fish Commission, which annually compiles and publishes its list of Florida's endangered species—fauna whose numbers have so declined that they are in danger of extinction.

Two such endangered mammals, the Florida panther and the manatee, are known well by the public because of vigilant media coverage. Other endangered species, such as the Gray and Indiana bats, have lower profiles and are suffering declines because of stereotyping and because most citizens fail to recognize them. Florida species that are listed as endangered on both the Florida Game and Fresh Water Commission and the U.S. Fish and Wildlife Service numbered 31 in 1989. Their future looks dim unless immediate conservation measures succeed. The species are:

Invertebrates

Schaus' swallowtail butterfly
Stock Island tree snail

Fish

Shortnose sturgeon
Okaloosa darter

Amphibians and Reptiles

Atlantic green turtle
American crocodile
Leatherback turtle
Atlantic hawksbill turtle
Atlantic ridley turtle

Birds

Cape Sable seaside sparrow
Dusky seaside sparrow
Florida grasshopper sparrow
Ivory-billed woodpecker
Kirtland's warbler
Wood stork
Snail kite
Bachman's warbler

Mammals

Right whale
Sei whale
Finback whale
Florida panther
Humpback whale
Gray bat
Indiana bat
Key Largo wood rat
Key deer
Key Largo cotton mouse
Choctawhatchee beach mouse
Perdido Key beach mouse
Sperm whale
West Indian manatee

In addition to the "endangered" classification, the Florida Game and Fresh Water Fish Commission lists those species threatened with extinction or of special concern. The 1989 list delineates 26 animal species as threatened, and 44 species of special concern.

Numbers on these lists change as the numbers of species advance or decline. Occasionally, a species such as the previously endangered alligator makes a remarkable comeback. Alligators, now estimated to number one million, remain listed as a species of special concern.

Wildlife biologists wish there were as much optimism about Florida panthers and manatees. The Florida panther continues to rank as the most highly endangered mammal in the United States, according to wildlife biologists. Only between 30 and 50 of the big cats remain in the state. Similarly, Florida continues to be a perilous home to manatees. In 1988, a record 133 sea cows died in the entire nation, with 128 of those deaths occurring in the Sunshine State. Their total number is estimated at 1,200, nearly all of them in Florida.

Conservationists say that habitat destruction is the most common cause of species decline as Florida real estate is gobbled up for resorts, residences, and agricultural use. That same development has led to the increase in plastic products along Florida's waterways, and it has resulted in animals increasingly being strangled by plastic fishing line and six-pack holders, not to mention sea turtles who mistake plastic bags for their favorite food, jellyfish. ~

Living Around Manatees

Docile manatees are inviting to everyone, particularly divers. The slow-moving, grazing water mammals wile away their winter days in many of Florida's rivers.

The endangered manatee is protected by several laws. The Marine Mammal Protection Act and the Endangered Species Act (both federal laws) as well as the Florida Manatee Sanctuary Act all forbid the harassing, capturing, or killing of manatees.

The laws require that boats operate at idle speed (no faster than necessary to steer a boat) in manatee zones, never pass over a submerged animal, and remain 50 feet away from manatees at all times.

The law defines annoying or harassing a manatee as pursuing, holding, prodding, or stabbing the mammal. It is also harassment to separate any manatee from a group or any calf from its mother. And any activity that prompts manatees to leave an area is illegal.

Glossary

Acid rain—rainwater with a pH less than that of pure rain (5.6 pH) caused when air, sulphur oxides, and nitrogen chemically combine with rainwater to become sulphurous and nitric acids. Acid rain has been recorded throughout Florida, with the most acidic readings (4.32 pH) found in the northern half of the state.

Algal bloom—overproduction of algae growth that occurs when too much nutrition enters the water.

Alluvial—material such as silt or sand deposited by moving water.

Aquifer—a permeable geologic formation such as rock or gravel that is saturated with water.

Artesian—water captured underground in non-porous rock or other geologic formation. If tapped for a well, the internal pressure of the water may cause it to bubble up like a fountain.

Blackwater—the darkened appearance of some waterways caused when water drains through acidic woods and swamps, which leach tannic and humic acids.

Brackish—slightly salty. The blend of fresh river water that meets salt water at embayments or estuaries.

Discharge—the quantity of water that flows by or through a certain point within a specified amount of time.

Drainage basin—collection point of surface water that is carried off by a river.

Ecosystem—interaction among and between organisms and their physical environment.

Effluent—an outflow, often used to describe a discharge of pollutants such as chemicals or sewage.

Endangered species—any plant or animal species whose number has dwindled sufficiently to place it in jeopardy of extinction.

Estuary—the point at which fresh water meets the sea.

First-magnitude spring—a flow of 100 cubic feet or more per second.

Flood plain—level land that may be submerged by flood water. These areas may also be built up by clay, sand, and silt during a flood.

Gauging station—a device that measures a river's discharge.

Greenhouse effect—first proposed in 1861, the entrapment of heat by carbon dioxide in a greenhouse fashion. As carbon dioxide increases from the burning of fossil fuels and the shrinking forest lands, the earth is believed to be in jeopardy of heating to dangerous levels.

Groundwater—underground, saturated water sources that supply wells or springs.

Hardness—the amount of certain ions, such as magnesium and calcium, found in water.

Headwaters—a river's beginning, meaning its source and upper reaches.

Hydrology—the science of water, including its origins, distribution, circulation, and properties underground, on the earth's surface, and in the atmosphere.

Mangroves—vegetation that grows in tidal areas that receive both fresh and salt water. Their value to Florida includes erosion protection as well as serving as critical nurseries to small creatures, which in turn feed fish and sea birds.

pH—a scale whose values range from zero to 14 used to measure acidity and alkalinity. A reading of zero to 7 indicates the acidic end of the scale, while numbers from 7 to 14 indicate alkalinity.

Percolation—rate at which water passes down through permeable substances such as sand or rock.

Permeable—openings in rock or other substances that permit liquid or gases to penetrate.

Potable—suitable for drinking.

Reverse flow—a stream flow that temporarily reverses direction because of a high tide at its mouth.

Riparian—pertaining to the bank of a lake or river.

River—a flowing body of water.

Runoff—water that enters waterways from either surface or underground sources.

Second-magnitude spring—flow of 10 to 100 cubic feet per second.

Sinkhole—a cavity in the land's surface caused by the collapse of underground caverns.

Species of special concern—plant or animal species whose numbers are progressively declining, heading toward a threatened status.

Spring—a supply of water issuing from the ground.

Spring-fed—describes a river, usually clear, that receives spring water flow.

Third-magnitude spring—flow of under 10 cubic feet per second.

Threatened species—plant or animal species whose numbers are low enough to warrant careful consideration lest they become endangered.

Water management districts—five governing bodies responsible for water resources in the state of Florida.

Water table—level at which water stands in those wells that penetrate an aquifer deeply enough to hold standing water.

Weir—a dam placed in a river to raise the water level.

Wetlands—lowlands partially submerged permanently or temporarily by shallow waters. These areas are widely varied and include fresh, brackish, or salty waters. Some sources estimate that 20 percent of all threatened or endangered species depend on wetlands for sustenance.